William H. Nobles

The Nobles
Emigrant Trail

Ken Johnston

Copyright 2018 Ken Johnston

ISBN# 978-1-941052-31-0 Trade Paper

Library of Congress Control Number: 2018951746

All rights reserved.
No part of this book may be reproduced or transmitted in any
form or by any means, electronic or mechanical,
including photocopying, recording or by any
information storage and retrieval system
without written permission
from the publisher.

Cover Design: Antelope Design
Cover Photo: Larry Turner

J. Goldsborough Bruff drawings used by
permission of Huntington Library, San Marino California

With appreciation to Lassen Association (formerly known as Lassen
Loomis Museum Association) for use of many excerpts from Robert
Amesbury's book, *Nobles' Emigrant Trail*, copyright 1967.

PronghornPress.org

In Dedication

To my mother,
Clella Maydew Johnston,
who gave me the inspiration
and desire to research the past
and bring its history to the present;

to my children
Erin, Bonnie, and K.C.,
who traveled many of the
emigrant trails with me
in my search;

and to
my wife
Jo Johnston
for editing, formatting,
and bringing this book
into existence.

Peace and Happy Trails to All

Table of Contents

Preface..13

Prologue 21

William Nobles and the Discovery of
Nobles Pass in 1851..27

Driving the Nobles Trail...45

Driving the Nobles Trail: Black Rock......................49

Driving the Nobles Trail: Black Rock Point............51

Driving the Nobles Trail: Granite Creek.................53

Driving the Nobles Trail: Guru Road......................61

Driving the Nobles Trail: Alternate Route to
Granite Creek..63

Driving the Nobles Trail: Trego Hot Springs......................67

Driving the Nobles Trail: Coyote Spring............................71

Driving the Nobles Trail: Great Boiling Springs.................73

Driving the Nobles Trail: Smoke Creek Desert..................75

Driving the Nobles Trail: Deep Hole Springs.....................79

Driving the Nobles Trail: Smoke Creek Road....................87

Driving the Nobles Trail: Wall Springs...............................91

Driving the Nobles Trail: Buffalo Springs..........................93

Driving the Nobles Trail: Smoke Creek..............................99

Driving the Nobles Trail: Smoke Creek Meadows............105

Driving the Nobles Trail: Smoke Creek Station................111

Driving the Nobles Trail: Robbers Roost..........................117

Driving the Nobles Trail: Mud Springs.............................121

Driving the Nobles Trail: View Land.................................131

Driving the Nobles Trail: Shaffer Station..........................135

Driving the Nobles Trail: Roop Town – Susanville............139

Overland and Idaho Routes...143

Big Spring..149

Nobles Pass...151

Butte Creek to Sunflower Flat and Manzanita Lake.........159

Black Butte to Hat Creek...161

Butte Creek West to Hat Creek: an Alternate Route........167

Wells Fargo Gold—A Mystery?....................................173

Manzanita Chute to Battle Creek................................175

Viola Resort..176

Deer Flat..177

Battle Creek and McCumber Reservoir........................180

Big Wheels..181

Ball Mill...183

Shingletown..185

Charlie's Ranch (aka Charley's Ranch).........................189

Foot of the Mountain Station.....................................197

Bear Creek and Dersch Ranch....................................199

Millville Plains Road and Twin Bridges.......................205

Cow Creek and Fort Reading..207

Sacramento Ferry..209

Clear Creek...211

Canon House and Graves..213

Shasta City or Old Shasta...215

1851-1852 Nobles Emigrant Trail..219

Other Contributing Discoveries to the Route....................233

Early Hints of a Trail Through Smoke Creek....................237

The Cherokee Cutoff...241

Nobles' Return to Minnesota and Road Promotion..........251

A Confusion of Names: Col. William H. *Noble* and
Col. William H. *Nobles*..269

Epilogue...277

About the Author...279

Bibliography..283

Index...289

Nobles Emigrant Trail

Preface

  In the spring of our country's bicentennial year in 1976, Lassen Volcanic National Park received a grant to develop a Living History Program to highlight and present the historic importance of both the Nobles Trail, which goes directly through the Park, and the nearby Lassen Trail, which was named for the prominent California pioneer who gave his name to the trail, to the Park, and to innumerable other places in Northern California.

  The grant provided for the purchase of a covered wagon, accouterments and equipment appropriate for pioneer emigrant travel, the rent or purchase of draft animals and a corral, period costumes, and a Hawken .50 caliber rifle.

  I had previously worked as a seasonal naturalist and park service ranger/interpreter at Lassen for four summers, working in the museum, leading hikes, and giving campfire talks. Then I had opted to work the following summer as

KEN JOHNSTON

a ranger at Denali National Park in Alaska. I enjoyed the experience and time spent there, but I missed being closer to my family and the friendships I'd formed at Lassen.

So, I was delighted when Lassen National Park's Chief Park Interpreter Richard (Dick) Vance called to offer me the job of developing a pioneer trails interpretive program. It sounded challenging and intriguing, as I had horses of my own, enjoyed working with draft animals, and was fascinated with the pioneer history of the trails. It also allowed my then four-year-old son, Erin Scott Johnston, to accompany me every day as a junior volunteer in the Park.

I told Dick that I would be glad to use my horses. I told him that I knew Marvin Fundenberger of Colusa, California, who had a couple outstanding oxen that I was sure he would be willing to lease to the Park for the summer. The oxen had brass knobs on their horns and were very gentle. They would be great for the program. Dick agreed and we started getting the program ready. We had the maintenance department build corrals and a shed for hay in the old Summertown service area located beside the Nobles Trail.

That first summer, we set up the program at Sunflower Flat, an open area about a mile up the trail, across the rugged landscape of the Chaos Jumbles and through a forested area. It was a location where the trail crossed the Park highway, and where tourists would see the camp, become curious, and stop for the program.

It was a short daily commute for us. I rode horseback leading the oxen, and my son, Erin, was able to ride with me on his Shetland pony, Lightning.

Arriving at Sunflower Flat, we tied the oxen to the wagon wheels, fed the animals hay, built a campfire, put on a pot of pennyroyal (picked fresh in the meadow) tea, and

Nobles Emigrant Trail

cooked Dutch oven biscuits to demonstrate life on the trail to tourists who stopped by. I then told them about the oxen and of the development of the California Trails, resulting in the finding of the Lassen and Nobles trails and the role they played in western migration and the Gold Rush.

This we did all day until quitting time, usually around 3 p.m. Then we led the oxen back down the trail to the corral where we fed them and the horses for the night. In following years, we converted from this casual drop-in arrangement and developed a more structured program with a main presentation at 1:00 p.m. every day. We moved the wagon to a place near Manzanita Lake Campground. In the morning, Erin and I would ride through the campground, stop at each campsite, speak with the people there, and invite them to the Pioneer Program in the afternoon.

Author resting at Sunflower Flats, Lassen Volcanic National Park
Photo courtesy of Author

KEN JOHNSTON

When the people arrived, a ranger in uniform would meet them at the amphitheater and hike with them through the woods to the location of the wagon. During the hike the ranger's talk would take them back in time to the mid-1800s, setting the scene for the program.

As they neared the location where the wagon was and the oxen were tied, Erin and I would gallop out of the trees, fire the Hawken rifle into the air, and appeal to the people to come to our aid. We would then lead them to the oxen and tie up our horses. Then I talked to the crowd about the oxen. I explained what they were, how the animals were used, and discussed the advantages of the pioneers' use of oxen over horses as draft animals.

I enlisted volunteers to help yoke the oxen, hook them to the wagon, and pull it to our campsite where we had a campfire prepared. Volunteer women in period costumes would prepare biscuits and put them in a Dutch oven while I started the fire and began my presentation. The women would then take young children off into the woods, seat them on logs, and tell them children's stories.

I baked the biscuits in the fire and told the history of the development of the western trails. I began with the use of the Oregon Trail, then explained the branching off of the California Trail, outlined its various branches, followed by the ultimate development and use of the Lassen Trail, and ending with the shortening of it by using the Nobles Route, which came directly through the Park near where we were at the moment, and ended at Shasta City.

At the end of the program, the women would bring the kids back. We then opened the Dutch oven, passed out fresh, hot biscuits to the people, and answered questions. After the crowd left, we extinguished the fire, put away the props, and led the oxen back to the corral.

NOBLES EMIGRANT TRAIL

It was a very popular program, and my son and I continued doing it for four very rewarding years. I am proud to say that the Pioneer Program is still in operation, if however, without the horses and oxen. Public health safety concerns now also prevent the actual cooking and handing out of biscuits. But, the program remains a popular event in the Park and presents important information to the public.

When my tenure at Lassen National Park ended, I retained my passion for the trails by doing historical

Cover of Legendary Truths:
Peter Lassen & His Gold Rush Trail in Fact & Fable

KEN JOHNSTON

Author doing a Living History program on Nobles Trail
in Lassen Volcanic National Park in 1976
Photo courtsy of Author

Nobles Emigrant Trail

research, following various trails across the country, and visiting museums and libraries related to the trails. Ultimately, I published *Legendary Truths, Peter Lassen and His Gold Rush Trail in Fact and Fable*, in which I attempted to address the inconsistencies that continued to be spread about that prominent pioneer and his trail.

I also became an active member of the Oregon California Trail Association (OCTA), and Trails West, Inc., two outstanding organizations dedicated to the locating, marking, and preservation of the historic trails.

Trails West, Inc. has published *A Guide to the Nobles Trail* with maps, pioneer emigrant quotes, and descriptions of the trail starting at the Black Rock, continuing on to Susanville, through Lassen National Park, and ending at Shasta City. It has locations and GPS coordinates of all the steel T-rail markers that are placed at significant points and stops along the trail. Following the Guide enhances the experience of exploring the route and brings the history and experiences of the emigrants who used the trail vividly to life.

Robert Amesbury, a dentist who lived in Susanville, California, authored the only other book written about the Nobles Trail. Mr. Amesbury was familiar with and passionate about its history. It was published in 1967 and gave an interesting description of the trail and the historical stories that happened along the route.

Although it may still be found in some libraries, it has long been out of print. That is the reason this book has been conceived—to preserve that history and also to bring it to the attention of modern day enthusiasts of history and the emigrant trails. History aficionados—those self-proclaimed "Rut Nuts" or "Trail Buffs"—beware. The trails can become addictive!

KEN JOHNSTON

Nobles Emigrant Trail

Prologue

All of the western emigrant trails leading to various destinations have their own legends, mysteries, tales of hardship, and promises of the advantages their use provided. It took many years of western expansion, exploration, route finding, and trail development, including road improvements and finding shortcuts—or "Cutoffs" as most were called—to develop the California Trails System.

The Nobles Trail was one of the latecomers, not appearing until 1852, after the Donner Tragedy, the Death Valley misadventure, the '49ers rush for gold, and the Lassen Trail's unrecognized role in saving thousands of late arriving "Greenhorns."[1] The Lassen Trail auspiciously took the

---

1 1849 was known as the year of the Greenhorn because thousands of people including doctors, lawyers, school teachers, family men from the cities set out on the trail without the experience and knowledge of trail life that emigrants in previous years possessed. They traveled too slowly and arrived in the West after the previous thousands of emigrants, with their livestock, had depleted the grass and needed resources along the older routes.

longer "round-about" that those inexperienced emigrants ungratefully (because of the hardships they encountered) called the "Horn-route" or "Lassen's Death Trail." In spite of the extra length, it ironically saved their lives.[2]

William Nobles pioneered the Nobles Trail in 1851. It provided a shortcut between the Applegate Trail in Nevada and the last section of the Lassen Trail in California, and was a much better alternative to the Lassen Route. In fact, it became what all the other trails to California would have wanted to become: shorter and more direct to its destination, with water and grass located in short intervals along the way, low elevation passes to cross the mountains, no steep ascents or descents to navigate, and a civilized destination where provisions could be obtained at its end.

In 1852, Nobles promoted the route's advantages over other routes, touting how it would benefit the merchants of Shasta City. He showed a delegation of men from there the route. In turn, he was paid $2,000 for his efforts before he returned to Minnesota.

His route later became incorporated in the Fort Kearney, South Pass, and Honey Lake Wagon Road. It received the first government funding for improvements of a western road, when the Minnesota legislature commissioned Nobles to present the route to the U.S. Congress. Through his efforts, Congress appropriated $300,000 for an expedition to evaluate and survey the route.

Frederick W. Lander was appointed superintendent of the expedition to map and improve the route. He opened

---

[2] Major Rucker, who was placed in charge of the government relief parties sent out on the incoming trails in 1849, reported, "Although the distance is much greater than by the old routes, and some of the emigrants were longer in getting in, I cannot but think it a fortunate circumstance they did so, for the loss of property would have been greater on the old trail as the grass would have been eaten off long before they could have arrived."

Nobles Emigrant Trail

several water holes and made improvements to the trail as he passed over it. His purpose for improving the road was the possibility of making it into a National Military Road.

It was briefly considered for a railroad route into California. It would arguably have been a better choice and easier to construct than the chosen route over Truckee Pass; however, the large population centers in central California, and therefore the political powers there, prevailed in getting the railroad.

Even so, the Nobles Route was extensively used until the 1870s, when it was superseded by the completion of the transcontinental railroad. However, the founding of Redding and Susanville resulted from its popularity at that time.

George Stewart, in his classic history of the development of *The California Trail, An Epic With Many Heroes*, made a statement that piqued my interest by its apparent inane-ness. He wrote that legends and tales told about Peter Lassen and his trail had "a ring of truth about them, at least of that legendary truth which sometimes comes closer to basic reality than mere history can."[3]

Fortunately, many of the emigrants on the trails west kept journals adhering to the dictum that "a life worth living is a life worth documenting." Men like John C. Frémont, Kit Carson, John Bidwell, Joseph Goldsborough Bruff, Alanzo Delano, Israel Lord, and many other early Californians and emigrants recorded and/or later recalled their daily experiences and observations. These have been preserved in libraries and historical archives for us to research today. It is this rich resource that has caused modern historians to investigate the "legendary truths" and to ferret out the facts.

Considering all the information recorded in journals and newspapers about Lassen at the time, I was thus

---

3 Stewart, George *The California Trail*. p. 213.

influenced to seek out the facts and disprove the legends and stories that Stewart claimed came "closer to basic reality than mere history can."

My efforts resulted in the publication of the book I mentioned in the Prologue. This said, I'll admit that in researching the history of William Nobles and his trail, I discovered that there was such a paucity of actual recorded information that, in his case, the legends and stories actually do have a better "ring of truth about them."

Amesbury's book cover. *Courtesy of Author*

Nobles Emigrant Trail

Trails West, Inc. Guide to Nobles Trail
Courtesy of Author

Much of the activities and travel of Nobles during the Gold Rush are presented only by stories. But some of the claims about his explorations, research of routes and passes, and what he was actually "the first to discover" can plainly be drawn into question and/or substantiated by journal entries and historical records that lead us into an intriguing inspection of the past.

The fictional character, Maxwell Scott, the newspaper editor in the movie *The Man Who Shot Liberty Valance*

KEN JOHNSTON

said, "When the legend becomes fact, print the legend."[4] Therefore and in some cases, the legends hold us spellbound and are well worth repeating and recording. However, in the following accounts I will attempt to correlate the actual written facts with the corresponding legendary accounts, and attempt to eschew any "alternate facts"that may turn up.

With that said, I must posit that the Nobles Trail itself remains perhaps the best Emigrant Trail for the novice, as well as for the seasoned "Rut Nut" and "Trail Buff" to experience and enjoy.

With the Trails West, Inc. *A Guide To The Nobles Trail*,[5] by Richard K. Brock and Robert S. Black, and a copy of this book, one may easily follow nearly the whole route (with the exception of a short section in the wilderness area within Lassen Volcanic National Park) of the Nobles Trail, from Black Rock to Shasta City, with a low-clearance, two-wheeled-drive vehicle. To do so offers the opportunity to: explore the myths, mysteries, murders, massacres, retributions and legal consequences of injustices that occurred throughout history along the trail; visit historic army forts, trading posts, stage stops, and emigrant resting places; relish the solitude and expansiveness of desert playas, towering mountain ranges, and volcanic landscapes; and challenge a part of our country that still remains one of America's most remote and rewarding.

Bon Voyage. Peace and Happy Trails,
Ken Johnston

---

4   John Ford, in *The Man Who Shot Liberty Valance*
5   Trails West, Inc. also has a pictorial guide to the Nobles Trail available at emigranttrailswest.org.

NOBLES EMIGRANT TRAIL

WILLIAM NOBLES AND THE DISCOVERY OF NOBLES PASS IN 1851

Innumerable mysteries and legends have shadowed the opening of the West, but recent clues and revelations have illuminated those shadows with compelling facts. Overland trail historians have been frustrated for years by the paucity of information about William H. Nobles. Little is recorded or known of his route into California, his activities and explorations leading to the discovery of Nobles Pass, his possible association with Peter Lassen, and his activities prior to presenting his "discovery" to the merchants of Shasta City in the spring of 1852.

For years, the "legendary truths," "imagination," and what "... old settlers of Indian Valley claimed,"[6] have

6 *Hutchings California Magazine.* No.32. February, 1859.

KEN JOHNSTON

shadowed the mysteries surrounding Nobles and his search for the mythical Gold Lake and the resultant "discovery" of the Nobles Trail. Tom Hunt in his introductory chapter to *A Guide To The Nobles Trail*, laments this frustration, and Dr. Robert Amesbury in *Nobles' Emigrant Trail* writes, "Time, in its relentless course has erased over which trail Nobles came to California," as he researched other facts.

Fortunately, research by these and other historians have revealed clues and resource information that lead to revelations of facts and conclusions previously unavailable. It is the goal of this book to reveal the clues and conclusions that have recently emerged.

Born in 1816 in New York, William Nobles was the son of a minister, Rev. Lemiel Nobles. He trained as a machinist and blacksmith and moved to St. Croix Falls, Wisconsin, in 1841 and assisted in building the first mill there. He later moved to Osceola, at the mouth of Willow River (later named Hudson). He was part owner of the Osceola mills in 1846, and it is claimed that he built the first frame house in Hudson. He moved to Stillwater, Minnesota, in 1843 and to Saint Paul in 1848.[7] He operated a machine shop there and did blacksmith work. He is reported to have built the first wagon in the territory. He married Susan Parker, and they had five children—three boys and two girls.

In 1850, Nobles joined the Gold Rush to California, but there is no record of the route he took, and there is very little information about where he went and what he did in California.

According to Robert Amesbury, William H. Nobles "...came into Honey Lake Valley or was guided by Peter Lassen with a band of 80 men in the spring of 1851. He probably heard and believed the story which Bruff recorded."

7 *Minnesota Legislative Reference Library Legislators Past and Present*
    https://www.leg.state.mn.us/legdb/fulldetail?ID=14177

Nobles Emigrant Trail

According to Bruff, that story recorded the year before was, "There were amongst us an individual who knew a man, who not long since traveling to California, started with 5 companions from somewhere about Mud Lakes (Black Rock Desert) leaving the emigrant road there to reach California by a cutoff—a diagonal beeline—and he found a lake deeply basined in the mountains with plenty of golden pebbles and hostile Indians near the headwaters of the Yuba."[8]

Legendary Gold Lake with shores of gold!   *Photo by Author*

Reports of this legendary and mythological lake led to a frenzied gold rush in 1850 and 1851. Thousands of miners, with hopes of filling their pockets with the gold nuggets that were said to lie on the shores of the lake, searched the mountains in vain.

The year previous to Nobles' arrival, Peter Lassen had spent the summer of 1850 extensively searching for the mythological Gold Lake.

---

8   Amesbury, Robert. *Nobles' Emigrant Trail.*, 4.

KEN JOHNSTON

Peter Lassen
Courtesy Lassen Volcanic National Park

He traveled from Big Meadows south of Mount Lassen, north around the peak to Cow Creek and Mount Shasta, then east to the present-day Alturas area, and south to discover Honey Lake Valley.

J. Goldsborough Bruff who accompanied Lassen as far east and south as the meadows where Smoke Creek Station would later be established on the Nobles Trail, recorded their travels and said that Lassen had been to Honey Lake on an earlier trip and had possibly gone to a lake somewhere to the east.[9]

Peter Lassen spent the winter in a large valley south of Big Meadows, which he named Caché Valley. He and Isadore Meyerowitz built a cabin that would serve as a trading post. They intended to raise vegetables and sell supplies to miners and prospectors entering the valley.

---
9   Bruff Journal. Oct. 1-3, 1850.

Nobles Emigrant Trail

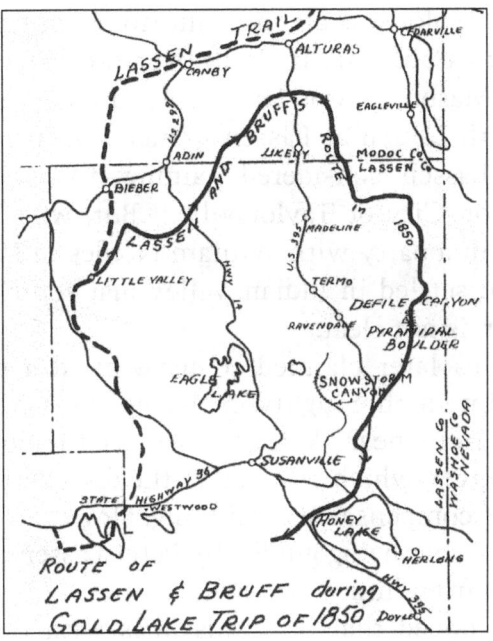

What was previously believed to have been Lassen's and Bruff's route in 1850. *Map drawn by Philip B. Lord and William Pratt*

Lassen was reported to have either guided prospecting parties or at least informed them of possibilities. *Many prospecting parties passed through the valley, including the Noble party in 1851. As Noble's party came over the mountain from American Valley and saw the abundant population of Maidu in the valley, they named it Indian Valley, which was quickly adopted. Among the 80 men in Noble's party was Jobe T. Taylor who later claimed the land now occupied by Taylorsville in February of 1852.*[10]

---

10   George, Holly, et. al. *Upper Feather River Watershed*

KEN JOHNSTON

Jobe Taylor was an emigrant from Pennsylvania who had come to California in 1849 over the Lassen Trail. He was also a Mason, as was Lassen. Apparently, he had some dealings with Lassen at Lassen's rancho in the Sacramento Valley, as Lassen considered naming his proposed town either Benton City or Taylorsville.[11] But, why Taylor later showed up in a party with William Nobles in Indian Valley in 1851 and settled in Indian Valley just south of Lassen's trading post, is not clear.

Nobles later claimed to have hired a couple men to assist him in thoroughly exploring the whole range of mountains from near Walkers Pass, in the south, to the Columbia River, which resulted in the discovery of the pass he later was compensated for finding. However, he made no mention of either being guided by Peter Lassen or of getting information from him.[12]

It is hoped that how this jibes with the stories of Nobles leading a party of eighty men, including Jobe Taylor, in search of Gold Lake, will be resolved by later historic research. Was Nobles interested in the gold when he went to Honey Lake Valley, or was he more interested in finding a cutoff? At any rate, according to Susanville historian, Tim Purdy, "At that point, Nobles and Lassen parted company."[13]

From there, Nobles must have explored the route through Smoke Creek to the "emigrant road at Mud Lakes." Thus, he would have scouted and confirmed the true "cutoff' that so many '49ers and Bruff had expected. However,

---

11 Wilson, General John. Letter to Peter Lassen from San Francisco, Jan. 3, 1849 (probably mis-dated, as it must have been 1850. Exhibit G in court transcripts.)

12 Read a more detailed account of Nobles claim of hiring two men to aid him in his search and an explanation of how much it would feasibly have cost him on pages 225-226.

13 Purdy, Tim *At a Glance A Susanville History*. p. 7 & 8.

Nobles Emigrant Trail

according to *Hutching's California Magazine* (June, 1857) at this time Nobles' proposed route would have met the Lassen Road at Lassen's Big Meadows.

These meadows were just to the west of what was then to become known as Nobles Pass.[14] Nobles then continued to Lassen's rancho, known as Rancho *Bosquejo*, following the established trail. Apparently, at this time he didn't know of the pass or route north of Mount Lassen providing a direct route into the Sacramento Valley and to Shasta City.

Not finding Lassen at his ranch, Nobles then traveled to Yerba Buena (later named San Francisco) to meet with Lassen at Henry Gerke's home. Gerke was a friend of Peter Lassen and a real estate developer in San Francisco. He later purchased Rancho *Bosquejo* from Lassen.[15] Also present at the time at Gerke's home were C.C. Catlett, General A. Hudson, I. L. Van Bokelyn, St. Felix, Messersmith, and others who would later testify to this.[16]

Nobles' intent was to present a business deal involving the establishment of ranches along his new route from the Black Rock, utilizing Lassen's ranch as the terminus in the Sacramento Valley, as it would "effectively give the proposed company a complete monopoly of trade along the route." There was mention of establishing ranches so they "might be able to turn a tidy profit." There was also mention of Nobles

---

14   According to *Fairfield's Pioneer History Of Lassen County, California.* P. 18, reference to the *Hutching's California Magazine* article:
"Lassen's Big Meadows was the west end of Noble's pass; and that the old settlers of Indian Valley claimed that to Peter Lassen is due the honor of having discovered the Noble's pass route, having known it long before Noble saw it."
15   Peninou, Ernest P. pp. 26 & 27.
16   Court Transcripts of Charles L. Wilson & John Wilson vs. Peter Lassen & Henry Gerke. October 5, 1853. Historic Records in Sacramento, CA. Witness Testimonies. p. 70 & 71.

asking for a "certain payment," from those wishing to profit from the enterprise, as he would later do at Shasta City. [17]

It is unknown if there had been any previous discussions about this with Lassen, but it is probable that Nobles had met with and possibly been guided by Lassen earlier in the summer.

In the words of Ruby Swartzlow, "He [Lassen] was consulted by soldiers, travelers, and emigrants because they relied on his familiarity with the terrain."[18]

Tom Hunt wrote, "Furthermore, both men had to have been active in the same geographical area in the early 1850's. It is hard to imagine Nobles, who was determined to open a new and better route into California, not searching out Lassen and availing himself of that trail pioneer's store of knowledge."[19] Plus, the presence of Jobe Taylor with Nobles highly suggests a connection to Lassen.

> *Hutchings California Magazine* claimed,
> *Most persons are well aware...[of] the emigration on what is known as Noble's Route—(Peter Lassen however it is claimed by the old settlers in Indian Valley, is entitled to that honor, having known it long before Mr. Noble ever saw it, and moreover was his guide all through this route, Mr. N. being entirely unacquainted with it.) This Mr. Lassen himself solemnly affirmed in our hearing, and so to us; and we make*

---

17   Quotes from Tom Hunt's essay in Brock, Richard K.; Black, Robert S.; and Buck, Donald E., et al. *A Guide to the Nobles Trail.* p.6.
18   Swartzlow, Ruby. *Lassen, His Life and Legacy.* p. 74.
19   Tom Hunt's essay in *A Guide to the Nobles Trail.* Op. Cit. p. 5.

Nobles Emigrant Trail

mention of it now that honor may be given where honor is most due.[20]

Lassen was apparently at Gerke's to get help in clearing his legal entanglement with the Wilsons and their earlier fraudulent attempt to purchase his ranch. He was interested in trying to enlist this group of men to help in ousting the Wilsons from his ranch. During the meeting, he produced papers, which were read over. But the others were unable to help with the entanglement.

Ultimately, Gerke purchased the rancho from Lassen. It is in the court transcripts from a lawsuit brought by the Wilsons against Lassen and Gerke that much has been revealed about Nobles and his activities before going to Shasta City.

According to Don Buck and Tom Hunt, "Nobles and the others could not satisfy Lassen's request to get rid of Wilson, so the deal collapsed." Because of this, or for some other reason, Nobles decided to further his explorations and take his road around the north side of Mount Lassen and end it at Shasta City, rather than at Lassen's ranch. To do this, he later met with Lassen at Rancho *Bosquejo* to explore the route.

Lassen had been around the north side of the "Snow Buttes" (Mount Lassen) in 1846 when guiding Lieutenant Gillespie to Klamath Lake with orders from Washington for Frémont to return to California and become involved in the Bear Flag Revolt. Lassen had also been around the north side of the "Snow Buttes" in 1850 when searching for the mythological Gold Lake, so he was already quite familiar with the landscape there.

When Mr. Pomeroy testified and was cross-examined during the Wilson vs. Lassen and Gerke Trial, he referred

---
20 *Hutching's California Magazine.* June, 1857

to his bookkeeping at Lassen's Rancho and expenses for the exploration of the pass over the mountains. He stated:

> ...*Mr. Lassen was charged at his own request with the board of the exploring party with the exception of Gerke. He said he did not want Gerke charged anything as he was a particular friend of his and that he always stopped at his (Gerke's) house when down at San Francisco with out any charge being made for it."*[21]
>
> *I think he [Lassen] left again in February and was gone only a few days he was to explore a new pass.* [Remember, Nobles Pass was east of Mount Lassen and ended at Lassen's Big Meadows].[22] *The party consisted of Lassen, Noble, Gerke, Hudson, Van Bokelyn, Smith and St. Felix. This was February 1852. The business of the party was to explore a new route through the mountains... it was about the time that Gerke & Noble arrived. I think Gerke came up on the second trip of the Comanche....*[23]

---

21 Court Transcripts of Charles L. Wilson & John Wilson vs. Peter Lassen & Henry Gerke. October 5, 1853. Historic Records in Sacramento, CA. Witness Testimonies. p. 68.
22 According to *Fairfield's Pioneer History Of Lassen County, California*. P. 18, in reference to the *Hutching's Magazine* article "'Lassen's Big Meadows,' was the west end of Noble's pass."
23 Court Transcripts of Charles L. Wilson & John Wilson vs. Peter Lassen & Henry Gerke. October 5, 1853. Historic Records in Sacramento, CA Witness Testimonies. p. 66 & 67.

Nobles Emigrant Trail

Lassen's Rancho Bosquejo.
This item is reproduced by permission of The Huntington Library, San Marino, California

Shasta City
Courtesy of Shasta State Historic Park

Later in the spring of 1852, after Lassen led the "exploring party" to find the "pass" through the mountains, no record remains of Nobles' activities after the party returned, until later in the spring when Nobles went to Shasta

City on April 17. He placed a notice in the *Shasta Courier* announcing a public meeting he would hold to present his proposal about his newly discovered route for a viable wagon road from the Humboldt River to their thriving town.

Nobles planned to show the businessmen of Shasta City the new wagon route for the consideration of $2,000.

That route initially branched off the Applegate Trail at Black Rock and headed southwest across the Black Rock and Smoke Creek Deserts to Honey Lake Valley and Susanville.

From Susanville, the trail continued westerly, up the Susan River (allegedly named to honor Nobles' wife), and over Nobles Pass, to where it intersected the Lassen Trail, followed it north to Feather Lake, through forested and volcanic country, and crossed the mountains on the north flank of Mount Lassen. Finally, it descended into the upper end of the Sacramento Valley, near Fort Reading, and terminated at Shasta City.

Nobles described the trail as easy to ascend, with water every eleven miles, and having abundant grass. The Nobles Trail would become one of the easiest of all the wagon routes into northern California, because, in the words of Will Bagley, "The gradual approach to Nobles Pass did not require an ox to do the work of a mountain goat."[24] So, it would receive heavy use in subsequent years.[25]

The April 17 *Shasta Courier* outlined Nobles' proposition to a large number of people in relation to the route:

> Mr. Nobles said: *With the assistance of the citizens of Shasta, I propose to open a good wagon road from this place to the Humboldt*

---

24 Bagley, Will. *With Golden Visions Bright Before Them.* p. 374.
25 The Nobles Trail was designated as part of the California National Historic Trail by Act of Congress in the 1992 Pony Express and California National Historic Trails Act. For more information on the trail, go to www.blm.gov/ca/st/en/fo/eaglelake/nobles.html

Nobles Emigrant Trail

river. For the sum of $2,000 I will indicate a route across the Sierra Nevada to the Humboldt river, which will be shorter and in every respect more practicable than any other known overland immigrant route into California. I would charge nothing for making the proposed route were it not for the fact that I have spent some money and much time in making its discovery. If, however, a company is sent with me, and should be dissatisfied with the road when they reach the eastern slope of the Sierra Nevada Mountains, I shall not consider myself entitled to any remuneration whatever.

I propose to take a party that may be selected to accompany me to the Truckee river, by a route which shall not vary ten miles from a direct course. The mountains are easy of ascent, and in no case will double teams be required to accomplish their passage. The snow upon the mountains is not of sufficient depth to prevent the travel of the road during the last portion of the month of April. In no instance are watering places on the route at a greater distance apart than eleven miles, and the grass abundant. The travel saved to the wearied immigrant will be at least two hundred and fifty miles over any other known route.

The point where the line of this route will intersect the Humboldt river is about sixty miles above the sinks of that river, and very nearly on the same parallel of latitude with this place. From this place to Humboldt river by the proposed, the distance is not more than two hundred and fifty miles. I have traveled the distance in eleven

KEN JOHNSTON

days, and believe it can be easily accomplished in eight.

On the route there are many desirable points for ranches, toll-bridges and ferries. If a company is formed for the purpose of opening the road, I shall ask an interest in one point of the road which I shall indicate. If, however, the public should take the matter in hand, they are welcome to all advantages that may accrue from opening the road.

I now leave the subject in your hands. I do not ask the payment of a cent for making public my route across the mountains, until those whom you may select to accompany me shall say that it is short and practicable for wagons.

Today, a bronze plaque on one of the old buildings in Shasta commemorates the meeting Nobles held.

Realizing the opening of a direct route through the mountains to the city would commercially benefit the city, the businessmen subscribed the $2,000 and hired Nobles to return to the Humboldt River and show them the new pass.

Several men, including: John Follansbee, Jack Hammans, John Dreibelbis, Charles Kyle, Mr. Swain, D. D. Harrell, W. Bonnafield, Samuel Francis, Dr. Thomas T. Cabaniss, Charles Smith, S. B. Knox, John Stratton, and Thomas Sheridan left Shasta on May 3, 1852 and returned later in June. They reported the route very satisfactorily fulfilled Nobles' claim.

They may have even elaborated a little, if not exaggerated, as reported in the *Shasta Courier* on 19 June 1852: "In many places on the route, indications of the existence of gold were observed. On the eastern slope, a vast amount of quartz was discovered. The party, however, were

Nobles Emigrant Trail

not prepared with necessary implements, and had not time, and are consequently unable to make any definite report as to the mineral resources of the country over which they passed. It is confidently anticipated, however, that rich deposits of gold will be discovered on the route."

When the party reached the Humboldt River, they remained there eight days. While resting there, a contingent of twenty-two men from Yreka passed on their way back east to St. Louis. William Nobles received his $2,000 payment from the Shasta delegation and started for his home in Minnesota with the new party.

> ON THIS SITE, IN MAY 1852, A GROUP OF SHASTA MERCHANTS MET WITH WILLIAM H. NOBLE TO EMPLOY HIM AS A GUIDE OVER A DIRECT ROUTE HE HAD MARKED AS AN IMMIGRANT TRAIL. THIS MEETING RESULTED IN THE ESTABLISHMENT OF THE NOBLE'S TRAIL.
> REDEDICATED APRIL 27, 1985
> BY
> TRINITARIANUS CHAPTER NO. 62,
> E CLAMPUS VITUS.

Shasta City Plaque
Photo by Author

KEN JOHNSTON

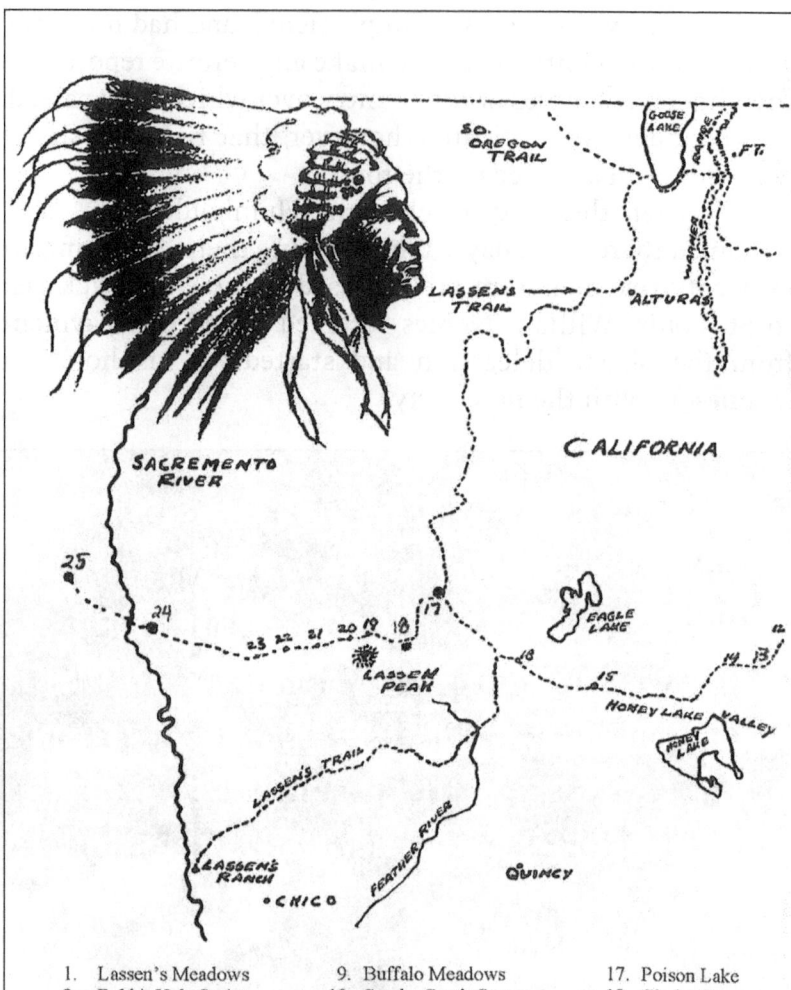

1. Lassen's Meadows
2. Rabbit Hole Springs
3. Black Rock Springs
4. Hot Springs
5. Granite Creek
6. Boiling Springs
7. Deep Hole Springs
8. Wall Springs
9. Buffalo Meadows
10. Smoke Creek Canyon
11. Smoke Creek Fort
12. Robbers Roost
13. Mud Springs
14. Mud Springs Massacre
15. Susanville
16. Big Springs
17. Poison Lake
18. Cinder Cone
19. Nobles' Pass
20. Deer Flat
21. McComber Mill
22. Ogburn Place
23. Dersch Place
24. Fort Reading
25. Shasta

Amesbury Map revised slightly

Nobles Emigrant Trail

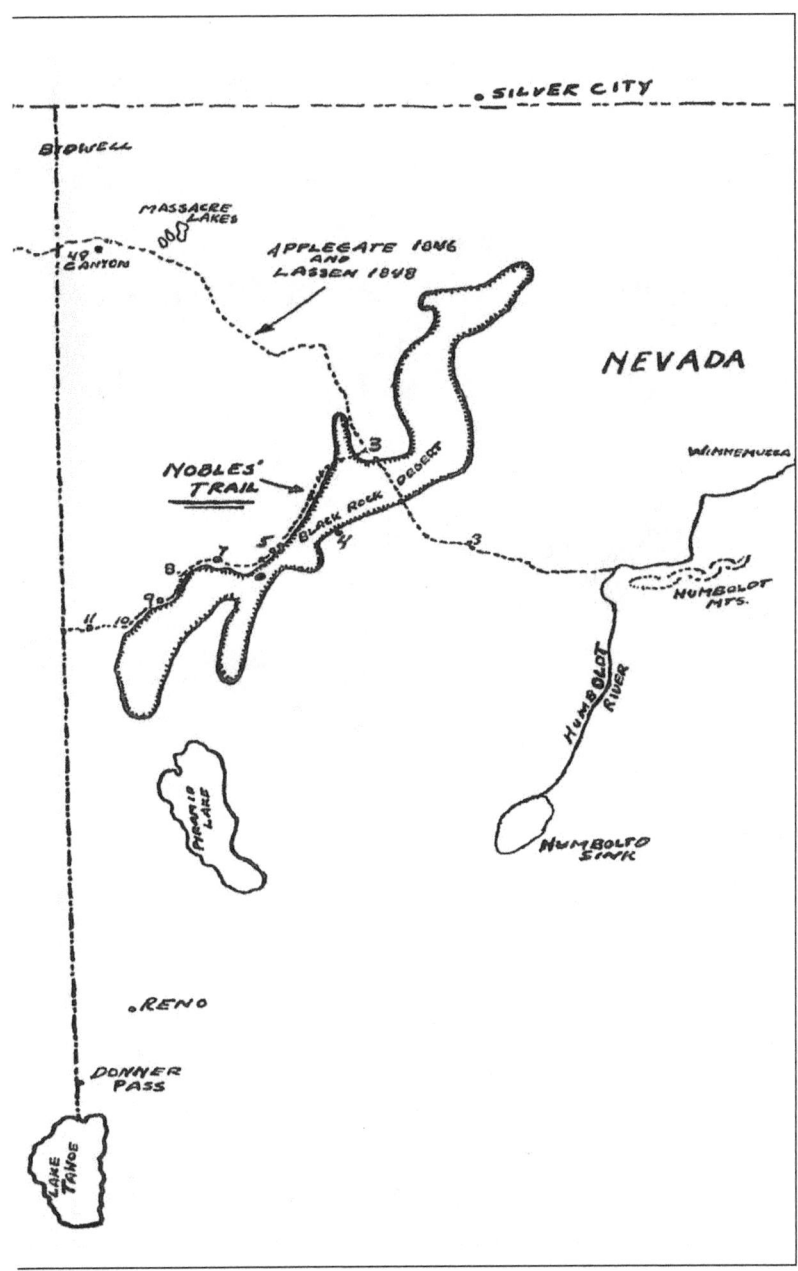

KEN JOHNSTON

Nobles Emigrant Trail

Driving the Nobles Trail

Robert Amesbury, in *Nobles' Emigrant Trail*, wrote:

> Before proceeding further with the history of the trail, it might be well to study the trail itself and learn more of it. One of the most interesting things about it is the fact that civilization has not erased this trace like the majority of the others which lie covered by railroads or have been blasted into oblivion to make way for freeways. There are many places in the trail where it has changed but little since the time John H. Dreibelbis passed over it in 1853 and wrote it up for **Hutchings California Magazine** *June 1857*. Fairfield states in history of Lassen

KEN JOHNSTON

County, the Nobles trail started at Black Rock point in Nevada. Of course, Nobles had to return clear to Lassen's Meadows to encounter the main stream of emigration along the Humboldt but his trail started officially at Black Rock Point. If one studies the map of this area it readily becomes apparent the wagons were again making a costly detour in traveling up from Rabbit Hole Springs to Black Rock and then back down the other leg of the triangle to Granite Creek when a direct line west from Rabbit Hole to Granite Creek is much closer and certainly more direct.

Amesbury's description remains true today. Driving the route presents Rut Nuts and Trail Buffs with fascinating glimpses into the past, around almost every corner and over nearly every hillock, not to mention the beauty of the landscape and opportunities to experience the openness and solitude in what remains one of the last areas of America's truly remote and wild West.

As you visit sites of murders and massacres, mysteries and intrigue, look for clues, watch for wildlife, perhaps catch sight of wild horses, donkeys, or other *ferae naturae*, and camp out under a desert sky that exposes the wonders of the Universe.

The route is open to travel by most any vehicle except in the most inclement weather, but be advised, you need to have good tires, plenty of gas, and let someone else know of your travel plans, as some areas are very remote and may not be in cell phone coverage.

Nobles Emigrant Trail

Trails West Inc marker N-1A
Photo by Author

KEN JOHNSTON

Black Rock Hot Springs
Photo by Author

Nobles Emigrant Trail

Driving the Nobles Trail:
Black Rock

Black Rock is not only the beginning of the Nobles Trail, it is also the destination for those with many interests. Every August, the population of the playa expands to more than 67,000 people who arrive for the annual Burning Man celebration, but at other times of the year people come to explore, experience, and discover the mysteries, wonders, and intrigues the area offers.

If we had arrived in this area 12,000 years ago at the end of the Pleistocene, we would have been amazed at the extent of Lake Lahontan. It reached a maximum depth of over five hundred feet above the playa and covered over 8,610 square miles of northwestern Nevada, with extensive stretches of open water separated by mountain ranges. Wave action created a series of wave cut terraces on many mountainsides that testify to the forces of the lake as it receded.

Its shores yield important clues about the high density of Paleoindian sites on its receding shores. Fossils of

KEN JOHNSTON

Pleistocene mammoths, giant ground sloths, camels, bison, and horses have been uncovered and can be seen at the Humboldt County Museum in Winnemucca and the Nevada State Museum in Reno.

Petrified wood and other plant fossils are common in the area, and a forest of Giant Sequoias grew here sixteen million years ago.

More recently, John C. Frémont, Kit Carson, and Alexis Godey explored the area. They were followed by the Applegates, Peter Lassen, and William Nobles, who pioneered emigrant trails through the area. It has been set aside as a National Conservation Area (NCA). It provides access to a unique combination of desert playa, narrow canyons, and mountainous areas—places where one can find solitude, camp in a wilderness beset by a universe of stars, and experience some of the hardships, pleasures, and daily challenges that the emigrants recorded in their journals as they made their way to Oregon or the gold fields of California.

It is our interest in these trails that has brought us here to Black Rock and the beginning of the Nobles Trail. We read a Trails West marker with two inscriptions, one on each side:

> APPLEGATE TRAIL–BLACK ROCK SPRINGS
> "WE FOUND THIS TO BE AN OASIS IN THE DESERT. A LARGE HOT SPRING, NEARLY THREE RODS IN DIAMETER, AND VERY DEEP, IRRIGATED ABOUT TWENTY ACRES OF GROUND– THE WATER COOLING AS IT RAN OFF."
> ALONZO DELANO AUG. 17, 1849

> "HERE THE ROAD CALLED NOBLES CUTOFF LEAVES THE OLD LAWSON ROUTE & TAKES A SOUTHWEST COURSE [TO GRANITE CREEK] OVER A BEAUTIFUL ROAD LEVEL AS A BRICK YARD AFTER YOU LEAVE THE BLACK ROCK SPRING ABOUT A MILE."
> J. D. RANDAL, AUG. 15, 1849[26]

---

26 Inscriptions on Trails West marker A-14 and N-1A.

Nobles Emigrant Trail

Driving the Nobles Trail:
Black Rock Point

The large black rock formation was used as a landmark by the Paiute peoples and later by emigrants crossing the area on the Applegate-Lassen Trails.

Arriving here in 1850, George Keller mentioned seeing:

> ...hundreds of ox skeletons between the Humboldt river and these wells (Rabbit Hole Springs) which had died the previous season from lack of food, there being very little good grass after the first of July. An hour's drive from the wells brings you to the desert proper – a vast plain destitute of vegetation. The stillness of death reigns over all – not the rustling of a leaf or the hum of an insect to break in on the eternal solitude. Man alone breaks it.

KEN JOHNSTON

Traveling north on the Lassen Trail and gaining a rise near Soldier Meadows, he was the first to allude to silver being found in this area by recording in his journal, "About 3 miles from the encampment we gained the summit of a bluff. There is said to be pure silver scattered over this." So the story obviously dates to, or possibly predates 1850.

Rumors later led to a "silver rush." About fifteen miles north of here, Peter Lassen was murdered in 1859 while searching for silver. A marker on the site is well worth the drive, and on the way you will pass the ghostly remains of Hardin City, which was later established to mine and process what proved to be the "elusive" silver.

In 1852, J.D. Randal wrote:

> *Here the road called Nobles cutoff leaves the old Lawson Route & takes a south west course over a beautiful road level as a brick yard after you leave the spring about a mile... This is entirely barren as far as the eye can reach in front & rear & I think about from 10 to 20 ms. wide. The mountains are very high all along here; and the stone have the appearance of cinder—after passing round the point of a bluff towards evening you will reach Granite Creek.*

Nobles Emigrant Trail

Driving the Nobles Trail:

Granite Creek

Granite Creek, claimed by some to be "twelve inches from hell,"[27] is located about five miles north of Gerlach, Nevada. It was the first water emigrants encountered on the west side of the desert. They were able to obtain water in a small canyon west of the meadow where their stock could feed.

The station had only two buildings and a stone walled corral, but it became a significant stopping place for emigrants and travelers in stagecoaches passing through the Black Rock Desert later. Here, they found a recruiting place for livestock, a campsite, a ranch, and a stagecoach stop.

In 1866, it became a military camp called Camp McKee, where detachments of soldiers were stationed to protect travelers on the Nobles Trail, later called the

---

27 Laura Sechrist, archeologist for Modoc National Forest in Alturas, CA, quoting Don Hardesty.

KEN JOHNSTON

Susanville to Humboldt River road. The military post was subsequently abandoned and moved north to Fort McGarry, now known as Soldier Meadows.

Remains of the stone corral and trading post built by Ladue Vary in 1856 is still visible, and ghosts of the past still linger from the violence that was described by *The Humbold Register* on April 15, 1865 as "The Butchery at Granite Creek Station."

Granite Creek Marker and trail
leading from the Black Rock Playa.
Photo by Author

Nobles Emigrant Trail

Remnants of Granite Creek Station
Photo by Author

Granite Creek flowing in the springtime.
Photo by Author

KEN JOHNSTON

On April 1, 1865, the Granite Creek Station was attacked by a Paiute war party. Two employees were killed in the attack while a third escaped, only to be caught and burned alive in what has come to be known as the Granite Creek Station Massacre.

According to Sessions B. Wheeler,[28] in March of 1865,

> "an Indian walked into the Granite Creek station on the edge of the Black Rock desert and asked for Lucius Arcularius. One of the four white men there, a visitor named Waldron, picked up a gun, put it up to the Indian's face, and told him to look down the barrel. When the Indian obeyed, the white man pulled the trigger.
>
> "A few days later burning revenge swept down upon the station and its three occupants—A. Curry, C. Creele, and A. Simmons. The April 15 issue of Unionville's Humboldt Register newspaper told of the hatred the red avengers brought with them...."

The article read:

> The walls of the house were built of thick pieces of sod. 10 loop holes for rifles had been made on the side attacked. The attack was made from a stone corral about 30 paces off in front of the house. The whole front of the corral is bespattered with lead of the bullets fired from the house. By appearances,

---

28 Wheeler, Sessions S. *The Nevada Desert*. p. 70.

Nobles Emigrant Trail

the fight is supposed to have lasted about half-a-day. Curry was killed by a shot through a loop-hole—a body found in the house having been recognized by persons acquainted with him. The legs, from below the knees, were missing.

The Indians must have exhausted their ammunition, for they fired long missiles before leaving, made from the screw ends of wagon bolts, cut about an inch long and partially smoothed. Two of these were found, one in a bellows near the house, the other planted two inches deep in the wood. Near the lodging place of the latter was a blood stain, and it is supposed the missile killed a dog belonging on the place—a savage animal intolerant of Indians. His skin was tanned, but left on the ground.

The Indians gained possession of a store-house, adjoining the dwelling, by tearing out a wall. The dwelling had a shake roof which they set afire. Then it is supposed that Creele and Simmons resorted to flight, taking that desperate chance in preference to burning.

They took their guns but didn't carry them far. Creele struck out across the flat towards Hot Springs. The flat is of alkali, very wet, and the tracks are left plain. Three Indians, two on horses and one on a mule, pursued and captured him. Brought him back to the house;

and all the indications attest that he was burned to death. A portion of the skull, a jawbone, and some small pieces of bone were found; the other portions of the body having been reduced to ashes. At the point where the arms would be, were large rocks piled up, everything indicating that he had been weighted down; and then a large pile of sawed lumber was built up over him—stubs of the lumber still remaining when these marks were found—and the poor fellow thus burned up.

Simmons took the road leading to Deep Hole Station. He ran about 30 or forty rods, and there the mark of a pool of blood denotes that he fared not quite so badly—having been shot down. The body was dragged off a short distance, and much mutilated. The remains of all the men, such as were found, were buried by this party on the 9th.

This was the beginning of Indian and military conflicts along the Nobles Trail. But, was the attack just in response to the shooting mentioned above by Wheeler? Or was it the result of years of minor conflicts between explorers, emigrants, and the Native Americans, who were given the derogatory epithet of "Digger Indians" when referring to Paiutes, Bannocks, and Shoshoni?

John C. Frémont, who passed through the area in 1844, wrote that the desert peoples he met represented "humanity in its lowest and most elementary state."

And, there were reports of Indians being needlessly

NOBLES EMIGRANT TRAIL

shot. Several trailblazers, Ewing Young, Joe Walker, and the son of Caleb Greenwood among them, had shot Digger Indians idly, for fun, or in punishment for theft.

So, the Indians definitely had cause for their retaliations—as did the whites. For example, many emigrant journals recorded incidents of attacks from ambush, where arrows would be shot to wound livestock that would then have to be left by the trail. They also reported instances of the natives stealing or pilfering even small items.

After this attack, the U. S. Army moved their camp from Smoke Creek Fort up to Granite Creek and, as stated before, established Fort Granite, also called Camp McKee, in 1866.

Another interesting incident occurred at Granite Creek Station and was recorded in Fariss & Smith's *History of Lassen, Plumas and Sierra Counties:*

> Hanging of Charles Barnhart—A case of summary justice occurred June 25, 1865 at Granite Creek, in a party headed by Captain Pierce of the firm of Pierce & Francis, proprietors of the Idaho stage line. This party had started out with a number of wagons and pack animals to work on the road to Idaho. On the morning in question Captain Pierce sent William Rogan to Charles Barnhart for a rope to be used in packing.
>
> Barnhart refused to give him the desired article, and when he laid his hand upon the rope to take it, drew his revolver and killed Rogan on the spot. There were present 30 citizens and ten soldiers and they at once formed

a court, tried him, Barnhart behaved in a most reckless manner, exhibiting that bravado that men of his class are pleased to call courage.

A gallows was improvised from wagon tongues, the prisoner was placed in position with a rope around his neck, and then asked to prefer a dying request. He said he wanted them all to get in front of him so that he could take a good look at them as he left. His request was complied with and he left immediately afterwards.

Ironically the murderer and his victim were buried in the same grave.[29]

---

29 Amesbury p. 20

NOBLES EMIGRANT TRAIL

DRIVING THE NOBLES TRAIL:

GURU ROAD

Just west of the highway and a little north of Gerlach is the legacy of an eccentric native of the town. DeWayne "Doobie" Williams, a Gerlach resident, is known as the "Guru of Gerlach" or the "Oracle of Gerlach."

Guru Road, also called "Doobie Road" or "Wonder Road," is a unique, desert-style art installation that was created in the 1980s and 1990s during the last fifteen years of his life. Using local stone and other found objects, Doobie crafted tributes to family, friends, and local residents.

Quirky installations and inscriptions have folksy sayings that are entertaining, and some may even require introspection. As one inscription says, "Remember No Matter What You Think of This Road the Price is Right."

The lane is about a mile long and has many philosophical and pseudo-philosophical "one liners," witticisms (some less witty and some quite weird) inscribed on rock cairns and naturalistic sculptures. If you have the time, it is a worthwhile excursion on the route south to Gerlach.

One of many exhibits on Guru Road.
Note the calcium carbonate rosettes that were
deposited by the receding Lake Lahontan.
These are commonly found around the playa.
Photo by Author

Nobles Emigrant Trail

Driving the Nobles Trail:

Alternate Route to Granite Creek

An alternate route later discovered to Granite Creek, beginning just north of Rabbit Hole Springs, not only shortened the distance, but it also avoided a longer drive across the desert that had caused so much trouble for earlier travelers:

> *Black Rock Desert. Just as the sun was sinking we resumed our journey, and after descending a little hill we encountered a country more forbidding...than even that I have already described...it was a country which had nothing of a redeeming character...a broad expanse of a uniform dead level plain, which conveyed to*

the mind the idea that it had been the muddy and sandy bottom of a former lake; and...the water had suddenly sunk through the fissures, leaving the bottom in a state of muddy fusion.
Jesse Quinn Thornton, 1846.

Sept. 1. Last water was rabit hole springs a poor place to water   had to go down in holes and dip with pails now here is the greatest wast of Property I ever saw wagons piled up and burned.
Sophia Helen Stone, 1852

Asa Fairfield and some references state that in 1856 Ladue Vary and Fred Hines discovered Trego Hot Springs when they took a shortcut from Granite Creek (now known as Granite Ranch) across the Black Rock Desert playa

Nobles Trail between Rabbit Hole Spring and Trego Hot Springs
Photo by Author

Nobles Emigrant Trail

towards Rabbit Hole Spring.[30] When they arrived at the Humboldt River, they met a wagon train turning onto the Nobles Emigrant Trail. Vary and Hines told the emigrants about the springs, the emigrants took the shortcut, and the Nobles Trail was adjusted accordingly. The notation, "Hot Spr," appears on the 1857 map of the Western Division of the Fort Kearney South Pass and Honey Lake Road at that location.[31]

However, Don Buck in his essay *The Development of the Nobles Trail*,[32] states that a shorter route to Granite Creek was made possible by the discovery of Hot Springs located on a direct shortcut between Rabbit Hole Springs and Granite Creek that was discovered as early as 1854.

Phoebe H. Terwilliger wrote on September 17, 1854 after leaving Rabbit Hole Springs, "… we took the right hand track [which] goes to Yreka [via the Applegate Trail] the other to Shasta [via the Nobles Trail] we came to Black Rock about sun an hour high found the great hot spring."

Terwilliger's journal entry proves a shortcut was known as early as 1854.

---

30 Fairfield, p. 35.
31 Wikipedia, Trego Hot Springs.
32 Don Buck essay in Brock & Black *A Guide To Nobles Trail*, p. 9.

KEN JOHNSTON

Nobles Emigrant Trail

Driving the Nobles Trail:
Trego Hot Springs

According to Carlson in *Nevada Place Names*, what the emigrants referred to in their journals as "Hot Springs" was named after the nearby Mount Trego (also known as Old Razorback Mountain) around the time the railroad was built in the early 1900s.

In 1844, Frémont passed by Trego Hot Springs, but due to fog in the valley didn't discover them. On January 6, he wrote:

> *The fog continued the same, and with Mr. Pruess and Carson, I ascended the mountain (Razorback) to sketch the leading features of the country, as some indication of our route, while Mr. Fitzpatrick explored the country below. In a very short distance we had ascended*

above the mist but the view obtained was not gratifying. The fog had partially cleared off from below when we reached the summit, and in the southwest corner of a basin communicating with that in which we had encamped we saw a lofty column of smoke, sixteen miles distant, indicating the presence of hot springs (Great Boiling Springs).

Trego Hot Springs   *Photo by Author*

Trego Hot Spring provided a more direct route to Granite Springs by not only reducing the distance traveled, but also by shortening the distances between watering holes, thereby making the desert crossing less stressful.

In 1860, Frederick W. Lander's group hand dug the four hundred foot long trench, improving the spring for animal use by emigrants, packers, and freighters, and also to water grass.

Nobles Emigrant Trail

Amesbury reports two 1861 entries from the diary of Edith Lockhart, who left Lassen's Meadows on the Humboldt and traveled to Trego Hot Spring:

> *August 18. Pleasant day. Started at noon and went 18 miles to Rabbit Hole Springs, rested a couple of hours and went 18 more miles by the next day to Hot Springs.*
>
> *August 19. A warm day - got into camp at 10 oclock in this morning, laid over till evening - when we went 12 miles to Granite Creek or Wells.*

Archaeological evidence shows the area was utilized seasonally by prehistoric peoples from 4,000 B.P. to 1,000 B.P. The hot springs continue to be used today for recreational purposes, but all hot springs are considered dangerous. It is impossible to tell how hot a spring is without testing it first before getting in. It is also dangerous to stand too close to the edge of a hot spring, because the banks are typically slippery and steep.

The Bureau of Land Management does not allow camping within three hundred feet of any water source.

Crossing the playa via Coyote Spring is the most direct route to Granite Creek, but the improved road goes west past another spring area that is also used for recreation. But it is on the private property of the Garrett Ranch. It is known as Frog Springs because, allegedly, bullfrogs were once commercially raised there.

KEN JOHNSTON

Coyote Spring with Granite Range in background.
Photo by Author

Nobles Emigrant Trail

Driving the Nobles Trail:
Coyote Spring

Coyote Spring was a seasonal spring about four miles west of Trego Hot Springs. It is located at a low sand mound that stands above the playa midway in the desert between Trego Hot Springs and Granite Creek Station. Care must be taken to be sure that the playa is dry, or it is possible to get stuck. However, in dry conditions this is the most direct way to Granite Creek.

KEN JOHNSTON

Great Boiling Spring
Photo by Author

Nobles Emigrant Trail

Driving the Nobles Trail:
Great Boiling Springs

Nobles Trail followed the Granite Mountains south past the Great Boiling Springs just north of the present town of Gerlach. John C. Frémont discovered the springs in January of 1844, when he and his party camped. He wrote, "Entering the neighboring valley, and crossing the bed of another lake, after a hard day's travel over ground of yielding mud and sand, we reached the springs, where we found an abundance of grass, which, though only tolerably good, made this place, with reference to the past, a refreshing and agreeable spot."

From this camp they explored west and south, finding and naming Pyramid Lake, and possibly contributed information leading to the route through Smoke Creek Desert later that was "discovered" by Nobles.

Just to the west of Great Boiling Springs is a Bureau

of Land Management (BLM) field office, where a small museum is maintained, and information about the area may be obtained. There is also an outdoor restroom that is always open.

The nearby town of Gerlach, just to the south, is the last chance to fill with gas or to buy a meal and supplies before you get to Susanville, California. Information and souvenirs can also be obtained at Friends of the Black Rock office in town.

NOBLES EMIGRANT TRAIL

Driving the Nobles Trail:
SMOKE CREEK DESERT

Continuing west on Highway 447, the road goes around Granite Point, the south end of the Granite Range, and through a low saddle, which is named Godey's Gap after one of Frémont's men. Alexander Godey was a hunter and guide with the Frémont expedition. He, along with Frémont and Kit Carson, explored south and west of Great Boiling Springs into the Smoke Creek Desert.

Jan. 7, 1844, Frémont left Gerlach Hot Springs. It is recorded that,

> ...he took Carson and Godey with him and they made a foray of the country ahead. By doing so, they found a ravine where there was good water and enough grass for an overnight stop. Also, there were cottonwoods for a change and a broad trail on which they saw tracks of unshod horses.

KEN JOHNSTON

During the next two days the expedition headed southwest, following what appeared to be a well-used trail.

To their immediate west, they saw a range of mountains (the Lake Range in Nevada's Washoe County) that had a fairly good covering of timber which Frémont thought might be cedar but which was really piñon pine. Pure water and a good covering of grass now became easier to find; and where there were springs, there were also groves of cottonwoods.[33]

It is unknown how far west they went, but it is known that Kit Carson crossed over the mountains to the south, allegedly over Emerson Pass at the south end of Smoke Creek Desert. Carson looked down and discovered a lake, then returned to get Frémont and show him the discovery, which Frémont would name Pyramid Lake.

It was for this excursion that Godey's Gap and Godey's Rock were named. Godey's Gap connects Black Rock Desert with Smoke Creek Desert, and Godey's Rock appears as a high ridge to the west and south of Gerlach.

Look for the sign for Planet X pottery on the south side of the highway—a must stop for quality pottery with a desert theme and an artistic interlude to your desert crossing.

A warning sign says, "Visit Planet X before it visits You," and a sign beside the driveway tells you that you are entering "Dry Creek National Pothole Preserve." The home of John and Rachel Bogard was an old homestead on the Nobles Trail that they have developed and where John makes his iconic pottery.

[33] Egan, Ferol. *Frémont, Explorer For A Restless Nation,* Reno, NV, University of Nevada Press. 192

NOBLES EMIGRANT TRAIL

Tosten Stabaek wrote in 1852, "Our path was now through a sagebrush plain, which made difficult going. At length we reached Deep Spring, where there were many springs and an abundance of grass for the cattle, and there we stopped until the following morning."

Planet X is probably the first of the "many springs" Stabaek was referring to.

Godey's Rock is the ridge behind Planet X
Photo by Author

KEN JOHNSTON

Deep Hole Station *Photo by Author*

Deep Hole Springs *Photo by Author*

Nobles Emigrant Trail

Driving the Nobles Trail:

Deep Hole Springs

Deep Hole Station was built in 1856 by Ladue Vary at the north end of the Smoke Creek Desert. The old stone trading post can still be visited, but it is on private ground. It became a major camping place and stopover with good water—and plenty of it—plus wood and grass on the Nobles Trail.

The area also became the scene of what Robert Amesbury claimed was the scene of much bitter Indian fighting. In July, 1869 two men were murdered at Deep Hole Springs. Bloody Point was named for this incident.

Robert Amesbury wrote:[34]

> *One man who was left in charge in 1862 while his companions went to Susanville for supplies was over come*

---

34 Amesbury p. 21 & 22.

by the Indians, scalped, had his head split open and his body was thrown into the spring nearby. This spring and a large surrounding area was later the base ranch of Louis Gerlach.

Fairfield has a detailed description of the deaths of Partridge and Coburn, in "The Murder of Partridge and Coburn, Told by Lafayette Marks and Others."[35]

During the spring and early summer of 1869 the station at Deep Hole springs, sixty miles east of Honey Lake valley on the emigrant road to the Humboldt river, was kept by Hiram L. Partridge, and Vesper Coburn worked for him. There were a few Indians who had belonged to the old marauding bands still roaming around in northwestern Nevada, and the friends of the two men had repeatedly warned them of the danger of staying there.

About the last day of July Christopher C. Rachford, afterwards Sheriff of Modoc county, who was coming in from Star City, arrived at Deep Hole. The door of the house was open, but there was no one around the place. He looked the premises over and found that the oxen and the wagon were gone. He then went down onto Squaw creek and there he found the wagon and the bodies of the two men. From their appearance he thought they had been

---

35 Fairfield p. 475 & 476.

Nobles Emigrant Trail

dead several days. (They were killed on the 27th of July.)

Rachford carried the news to Surprise valley. Olin Ward, for many years a prominent stock man of that section, said that Rachford told the foregoing to him. At the time of the murder and for several days previous to it a band of Piute Indians had been camped in Surprise valley, and had to the knowledge of the citizens, made two trips to Deep Hole springs; but no suspicion of hostile intentions were entertained, though signal fires were on the hills every night. The same night that Rachford reached the valley every Indian disappeared, and though the soldiers from Camp Bidwell sought industriously they failed to find them.

Probably the same day that Rachford was there a party of Honey Lakers, also coming from the Humboldt, reached Deep Hole late in the evening. Finding no one there they took possession of the place for the night. They thought it strange that the premises had been left alone and the next morning they began to look around. Before long they noticed a comparatively fresh wagon track going from the station out into the brush, and after following this some distance, Tunison says two miles, they found the dead bodies of Partridge and Coburn.

Judging from appearances, they had hitched a yoke of cattle to the wagon and gone after a load of sage brush for fuel, leaving their guns at the station. When they saw the Indians coming they went to the oxen, pulled the bows from the yoke and set them free, and then ran for home. They didn't get very far, perhaps a hundred yards, before Partridge was killed. Coburn got a hundred yards further and a bullet broke his leg just above the ankle. Even after this he must have tried to run, for the broken bone was forced through the flesh. When found he had a small knife, one blade of which was opened, tightly grasped in his hand. He was shot twice and Partridge five times.

The Honey Lakers took the bodies to the station and buried them and came on to Susanville. John C. Partridge, Hiram's cousin, Collins Gaddy, Lafayette Marks, and Cap. Hill immediately started for Deep Hole with a couple of buggies and two coffins. The bodies of the two men were brought to Susanville and buried there August 5th, Partridge being given a Masonic burial.

In an annual report by the Commissioner of Indian Affairs, J.M. Lee wrote of the consequential capture of the Indians thought to have participated in the murders. He also alluded to the cruel treatment and racial injustices the Native Americans were subjected to.

Nobles Emigrant Trail

In my annual report for 1869 under the head of outrages I detailed the murder by Indians of two white men Partridge and Coburn at Deep Hole Springs Nevada in July 1869. I investigated the case as far as possible and it appeared that the white men were killed by two Indians brothers Amazoo and Hop-we-puck-ee living in the northern section of the State.

Military authorities at Camp Bidwell California arrested several Indians suspicioned as perpetrators of the murder among the number Hop-we-puck-ee. He was finally turned over to civil authorities at Susanville California was taken from the custody of the constable by some white men and hanged in September 1869. Amazoo was apprehended near Reno Nevada together with two other Indians Joe and Mack who belonged on the reservation and who were innocent of any criminal knowledge or participation in the murder.

At a preliminary examination nothing was adduced against these Indians but instead of being released Deputy Sheriff Edwards turned them over without authority to some irresponsible white men from Honey Lake Valley California. These men took the Indians a few miles from Reno

> murdered them and threw their bodies into a deep hole by the wayside.
>
> Such was in substance the Indian version of these outrages and subsequent information has almost fully verified their statements. These cases illustrate the swift and unlawful retribution to which Indians in this State are subjected without any discrimination as to guilt or innocence A suspicion against an Indian is tantamount to his death warrant to be executed by bad white men without fear of prosecution or molestation at the hands of civil authorities.[36]

According to Amesbury, before Louis Gerlach purchased Deep Hole Springs and it became part of the Gerlach Land & Livestock Company, it had belonged to the vast Miller and Lux cattle ranch properties. This empire was so huge it was said that people could drive cattle from Oregon to San Francisco and bed them on Miller and Lux property every night.

Just to the northeast and across the road from Deep Hole Springs, the pointed rise extending from the Granite Mountains is still called "Bloody Point" to commemorate the killings of Partridge and Coburn.

A short distance northeast of Deep Hole Springs, you will turn left off Highway 447 and onto Smoke Creek Road, as the Nobles Trail roughly follows this road along the edge of Smoke Creek Desert to Smoke Creek. Just past this intersection, look north to view an excellent example of

---

36 J.M. Lee, Annual Report of the Commissioner of Indian Affairs by United States. Office of Indian Affairs, 1870

wave cut terraces carved into the mountains by the receding Lake Lahontan that covered much of northwestern Nevada at the end of the Pleistocene.

Wave cut terraces
Photo by Author

KEN JOHNSTON

Nobles Emigrant Trail

Driving the Nobles Trail:
Smoke Creek Road

According to John Evanoff in Nevada History,
There is some speculation that besides Noble and a few other notable emigrant guides, the southern Smoke Creek Desert area was also crisscrossed by Kit Carson. Carson was often sent ahead of John C. Fremont's main party to find Indian trails and a path south in the group's first venture to map the western United States in 1844.

A road paralleling the railroad tracks along the southern edge of the Smoke Creek Desert is a excellent four wheel drive trail for those who wish to explore the Terraced Hills north of Pyramid

KEN JOHNSTON

Lake and Emerson Pass where a few people believe Carson first saw the lake and then hurried back to catch Fremont heading south into the San Emidio Desert south of the Black Rock.

He told Fremont of the lake and after Kit was sent up a hill that still bears his name on many maps, they changed direction heading over San Emidio Canyon and down Sweetwater Canyon to eventually peer at the amazing body of water he later named Pyramid. They camped by the large pyramid shaped rock at the lake's eastern side and that reminded Fremont of the great pyramid at Giza in Egypt which he had visited years previously.[37]

Frémont did name Pyramid Lake, but this author has not been able to locate any record of Frémont actually ever having visited the pyramid of Giza.

As you travel down Smoke Creek Road, keep an eye open for wildlife, as we have seen feral donkeys, a badger crossing the road, many Golden Eagles, jackrabbits, coyotes, and other animals. The two wild burros in the picture belong to a herd of up to 150 reported in the area. Note the two dark specks at the top of the rock are Bald Eagles.

About four miles west of the turnoff, Indian Rock monolith will come into view about a quarter mile north of the road. It was formed by lava pushing up through surrounding rock and later eroded. While covered by Lake Lahontan, mineral laden water precipitated carbonate minerals called "tufa" around it. To the north of the rock

---

37   Evanoff, John C. *Nevada History.*

Nobles Emigrant Trail

is Indian Rock Spring, which has been a destination for sheepherders and their flocks in the past. How the Rock got its name is somewhat of a mystery, as none of the locals seem to know. One told me that there used to be "Indian writing" (petroglyphs?) on it but it has eroded off. Another just said, "Oh, it's the rock the Indians used to go behind to take a pee!"

Burros at Indian Rock with bald eagles on top of the rock.
Photo by Author

KEN JOHNSTON

Nobles Emigrant Trail

Driving the Nobles Trail:
Wall Springs

Wall Springs, about nine miles west of Deep Hole, is mentioned in several travelers' diaries. The trail here followed the northern edge of the desert along the foothills, but an alternate route traveled more directly toward Buffalo Springs when the playa wasn't seasonally impacted by mud.

According to Amesbury, "The spring was used extensively by the Army troops as they moved back and forth along this trail in search of war parties."

He also said that it was near the Wall Springs that Lucius Arcularius was ambushed by Indians in March 1865. "When he was shot, his horse ran with him about 100 yards, when he toppled off. He was stripped by the Indians and thrown into the grease brush. They took everything he had, and as his horse was not found, they probably got that too."

According to Raymond Smith, "Apparently he had

Trails West marker at Wall Springs
Photo by Author

been robbed and then killed by two men, but there was no proof that they were Indians. Regardless, the murder was reported and accepted as an 'Indian outbreak' which threatened the safety of all in the area, especially those traveling on the new mule and stage road from Chico to Silver City in Idaho."[38]

The springs provided "plenty of water, some grass & sage for fuel." Solomon Kingery on Aug. 4, 1852 wrote, "Encamped at monday Lake [Wall Spring]. It is about 4 rod in diameter. The bottom can not be seen. Water is good but a little worm (sic). Grass tolerable... The road runs in the Edge of this vally. It makes a very level & good road."[39]

---

38 Smith, Raymond M. *Nevada's Northwest Corner.* Reno, NV, Silver State Printing, p.44.
39 Brock & Black. p. 41.

Nobles Emigrant Trail

Driving the Nobles Trail:
Buffalo Springs

According to Amesbury, this area allegedly gets its name from Indian claims that at one time buffalo inhabited the meadow above the springs. But Brock and Black write, "Although buffalo herds didn't range into the arid Great Basin, there were isolated patches of native 'Buffalo Grass' which was dominant forage grass on the Great Plains. Apparently Buffalo Springs was named after this."

And in 1857, John Kirk wrote,
> Buffalo Springs...do not deserve the name of springs as they afford but a trifling quantity of sulphurous [sic] water, which slowly oozes from the black and filthy slime."

What does make this area one to be remembered is the salt works originally

KEN JOHNSTON

Salt Evaporation at Buffalo Meadows
Photo by Robert Amesbury dated 1967

Salt Works Smoke Creek Desert
Photo courtesy of Jim Watt of Gerlach 2017

Nobles Emigrant Trail

taken up by Frank Murphy and 'Comanche George' Lawrence in 1864. This salt works produced salt from brine wells for farm stock and mining as far south as Marysville. Its remnants can still be seen today on the edge of Smoke Creek Desert.[40]

In 1877, Thomas W. Symons traveled through the area. He reported:

> Leaving Surprise Valley we set out going through the old outlet of the lake by the main road to Reno and separating at Clark's about 10 miles from the valley two courses were run to the Granite Mountain which was occupied as our last triangulation station October 26; A four days march from Granite Mountain brought us to Susanville passing by Wall Springs, Murphy's Salt Works, Smoke Creek, and Shafer's.
>
> Mr. Murphy has built up quite an industry in the desert. On boring a few feet into the soil water is found which is a fully saturated solution of salt and which by means of a windmill he pumps into inclosed spaces of the ground and there it is evaporated and leaves the salt which is very pure and of excellent quality. From one gallon of water he gets two pounds and ten ounces of salt. He was extending his works so as to make more salt as he is at present unable to supply the demand.[41]

40 Amesbury, p. 23.
41 Thomas W. Symons, "Executive and Descriptive Report of Lieutenant Thomas W. Symons Corp of Engineers on the operations of Party No 1 California Section Field Season of 1877," p. 118, 1878.

KEN JOHNSTON

A Trails West marker stands just to the left of the ranch entrance, and the salt works are located a couple miles to the south and west on the playa. Visiting the area is not recommended, as the playa may be marshy and muddy.

Early journal entries reported Buffalo Springs was unworthy of the name because, as stated above, the water was "sulphurous...which slowly oozes from the black and filthy slime." But Fredrick Lander improved the spring in 1860 by sinking a well and installing wooden troughs to catch the water that percolated from the spring. Due to numerous improvements and alterations, the exact location of the original springs is not known.

Wild Horse Canyon entering the Smoke Creek Playa to the south gets its name from a herd of horses purchased in the early 1860s in San Diego. Frank Murphy and a business partner drove the horses north to this area, where they were turned loose in the canyon, giving it its name. Their descendants are the wild horses we see in the area today.

> *Many writers speak glowingly of these horses in later years as being the finest of the wild breed. Descendants of this herd were in later years driven to Amedee* [on the east shore of Honey Lake] *and shipped to the Boer War, the Spanish American War and still later, World War I. Thus, this exemplifies again that the horse, while never being angry at anyone, fought and died in more wars than any other animal."* Amesbury, 1967.[42]

Amesbury writes that before Murphy and Lawrence brought horses to Buffalo Springs and released them, the

---

42 Amesbury p.23.

Nobles Emigrant Trail

local Indians had been afoot, and it was later they learned to use them as mounts.

Across the desert to the south, the Fox Range rises between the playa and Pyramid Lake. Reynard Siding was established on the railroad there, and prior to 1917 the Western Pacific was considering building a light-traffic line from Reynard through Buffalo Canyon to the Surprise Valley near Cedarville in the north. Wikipedia states that "Reynard" was a literary figure in French, Dutch, English, and German fables. He was an anthropomorphic red fox and trickster. Probably the names for Reynard Siding and the nearby Fox Range share a common origin.

From Buffalo Springs (Trails West marker N-11), drive about seven miles south to where swales of the Nobles Trail cross the Smoke Creek Road at Trails West marker N-12. Here the trail goes over a rise to the west and drops into Smoke Creek Canyon. Continue south another mile and turn west on Smoke Creek Road at the junction with Sand Pass Road.

KEN JOHNSTON

Nobles Emigrant Trail

Driving the Nobles Trail:
Smoke Creek

Smoke Creek is a crystal-clear mountain stream that flows from the southern base of Observation Peak (7,964 feet) to the north of Smoke Creek Desert, and just over the California-Nevada state line to the west. The name reportedly derives from the dust devils that are frequently seen on this desert from the northwest. But Amesbury says it was named by Indians as they watched vapor rise from the creek in the morning.

The creek gives its name to the desert it flows into. On its way, it cuts through some steep-walled volcanic canyons and opens into a grassy valley that became an important stop for emigrants and freighters using the Nobles Trail. As you continue up Smoke Creek Road, you will be entering a steep-walled canyon carved by the creek. In 3.9 miles, Trails West marker N-13 stands in front of a large cave to the right and below the road.

KEN JOHNSTON

Trails West group at Cave in Smoke Creek Canyon
Photo by Author

In 1860, Mary Fish, traveling by the cave in the canyon, wrote, "... several of the company having entered on horseback but I do not think they saw much for it was dark as pitch in the cave I had some fears of Indians as this canyon was an excellent place for them to make an attack."

As you continue through the high-walled canyon, take time to stop, view, and ponder the formations coating the upper surfaces of the walls. In 1857, Superintendent John Kirk wrote: "This cañon is 2½ miles in length and varies in width from 30 to 150 yds, the sides are abrupt and in places 250 feet high. The formation metamorphis. In many places on the top of the walls I observed the cement coatings."

What you are actually looking at, and what Kirk was describing, is calcium carbonate tufa, an evaporite from the

Nobles Emigrant Trail

waters of the receding Pleistocene Lake Lahontan thousands of years ago. Being a land-locked or endorheic lake, like the Great Salt Lake, mineral concentrations formed as the lake waters evaporated and receded leaving evaporites along the shoreline, as you see here, and on lake bottoms like the rosettes found on the playas and displayed on Guru Road.

It is nearly mind boggling to realize that the surface of the ancient lake was five hundred feet deep over the Black Rock and Smoke Creek Playas, and its waters extended across this area into the Honey Lake Valley. Notice also the wave-cut terraces in the surrounding mountainsides.

Just up the canyon, it becomes narrower. Wagon travel was impeded by a dense growth of willows, so the trail crossed the creek and turned west passing up and onto a shelf, thus bypassing the obstruction. In a couple miles, the trail drops down off the shelf and re-crosses the creek.

Trails West marker N-14 states:

NOBLES TRAIL–SMOKE CREEK BYPASS
"THICK WILLOWS ARE IN THE WAY OF PASSING EASILY UP THE STREAM, WHICH IS FOLLOWED, HOWEVER, BY A WAGON-ROAD FOR A MILE, WHICH THEN LEAVES IT AND PASSES OVER THE HILLS ON THE SOUTH SIDE TO THE HEAD OF THE GORGE."
-LT. E. G. BECKWITH, JUN 21, 1854

From here, the Smoke Creek Canyon opens into a wide, grassy valley watered by the confluence of Smoke Creek and Rush Creek from the west. It provided ample feed and water for emigrants and freighters following the Nobles Trail, and it became the site of Smoke Creek Station, military Camp Pollock, and present Smoke Creek Ranch. The history and prehistory of the area provides much substance for interesting research and reading.

Tufa deposit on canyon rim.
Photo by Author

Nobles Emigrant Trail

Trails West marker N-12 Descent of swale to Smoke Creek
Photo by Author

KEN JOHNSTON

Nobles Emigrant Trail

Driving the Nobles Trail:

Smoke Creek Meadows

In addition to the fascinating geologic history of Smoke Creek, Native Americans have occupied the area since time immemorial. They lived and hunted here. In the canyons to the north they inscribed petroglyphs that were first sketched and documented in 1850 by J. Goldsborough Bruff, who was a member of Peter Lassen's prospecting party searching for the mythical Gold Lake, whose shores were allegedly lined with gold nuggets.

On October 1, 1850, Bruff drew sketches of the petroglyphs, most notably ones of a pyramid rock in the canyon a few miles upstream from here. He noted in his journal, "I pictured several of the most distinct groups of symbols, and some look much like the Egyptian; But was compelled to have a friend at my elbow, with ready rifle, to look out for the Philistines (Indians) while I sketched."

Pyramid Rock in Smoke Creek Canyon
Photo by Author

NOBLES EMIGRANT TRAIL

Bruff's Drawing of Pyramid Rock
*This item reproduced by permission of The Huntington Library,
San Marino, California*

KEN JOHNSTON

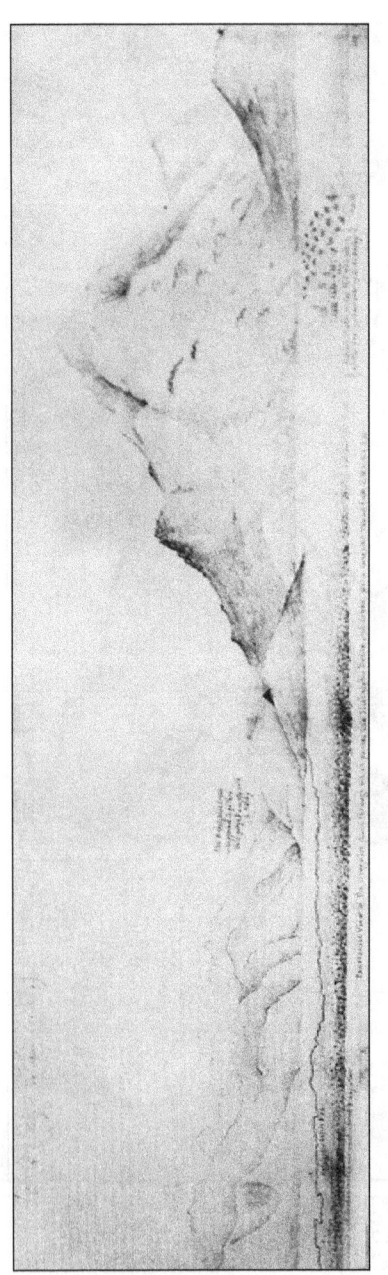 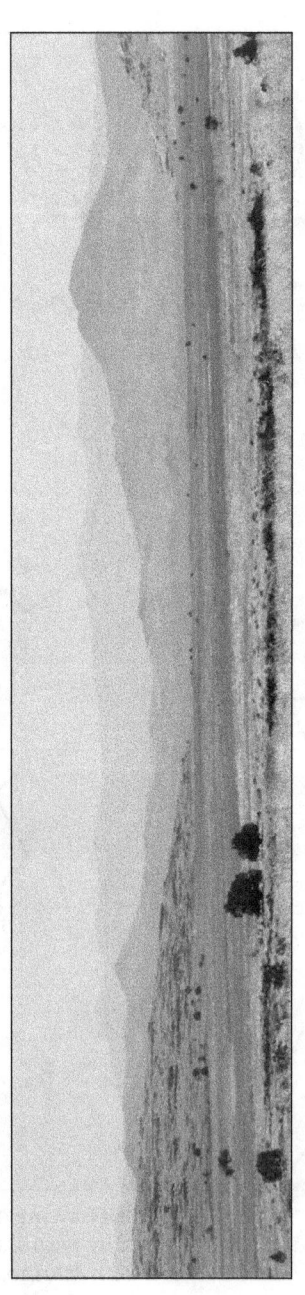

Bruff's panoramic sketch on left. Compare to photo of Smoke Creek Valley with the mountain and "defile" to the east and south, flowing into Smoke Creek Desert beyond. *Bruff's sketch reproduced by permission of The Huntington Library, San Marino, California. Photo by Author*

Nobles Emigrant Trail

They then continued to ride down the canyon he named *"Heioglyphic Defile & creek."*[43] He then wrote,

> *Kept S. over a very stony plain, with scattered sage, and gradually descended to a meadow of grass & marsh, with rills and water holes. It runs along the base of a mountain range – to the S.E. Here we camped, on a tolerable dry grassy place, alongside a marsh. The mountain range near us, rises to a very high peak, and a gap in the hills – which run E.N.E.*

They camped in this meadow, where Bruff drew a panoramic sketch of the camp, the mountain in the background, and the "Heioglyphic Defile" he noted to the south and east of the mountain and their camp. Comparing the sketch to a photo of the site (on the opposite page) confirms that it was in this place they camped.

They then traveled west and south to enter Honey Lake Valley, basically following the route the Nobles Trail later would. Bruff indicated that Lassen had visited this area earlier, but it isn't known if Lassen traveled farther east.

Bruff also mentioned seeing abundant horse and mule tracks. The following day, after traveling some distance, he saw more tracks and wrote, "Plenty of horse & mule tracks, and manure, not over 10 months old."[44]

Since it is doubtful that the local Paiutes used horses or—especially—mules that early, this suggests that packers during the Gold Rush of 1849 (ten months earlier!) may have traveled this way. At least, some journals written in 1849 alluded to a shortcut, and some referred to a "Cherokee Cutoff." Could the horse and mule tracks have been from

---

43 The term, petroglyph, wasn't used until 1877. But Bruff had seen images of Egyptian hieroglyphics.

44 Read, Georgia Willis and Ruth Gaines, eds. p. 829.

the Cherokee pack train led by Dick Owens in 1849? Could they all have been following the same ancient Indian trail from Smoke Creek to Honey Lake?

As you drive into the meadow where the canyon opens up, look toward the base of the mountain to the west for a white cross in front of a cliff. It stands above the site of Smoke Creek Station and is before you come to the actual area where Bruff camped and sketched the panorama.

Smoke Creek Cross
Photo by Author

NOBLES EMIGRANT TRAIL

DRIVING THE NOBLES TRAIL:
SMOKE CREEK STATION

Traveled 19 miles and camped on Smoke Creek. Grass good, water poor, Plenty dry willows. Road for the first 5 miles nearly level and good. The next 5 miles we traveled over hills many of which were high steep and stony and some of them sandy....Road after dinner in a canyon much of it very stony. There is a trading post close by just back of camp....Allen J. Tyrell, September 4, 1860 Journal entry

On Smoke Creek, just east of the Nevada state line, T.P. Kingsbury opened a store in May of 1857, which catered to travelers on the Nobles Road. Around the station were large grazing areas and plenty of water for an important

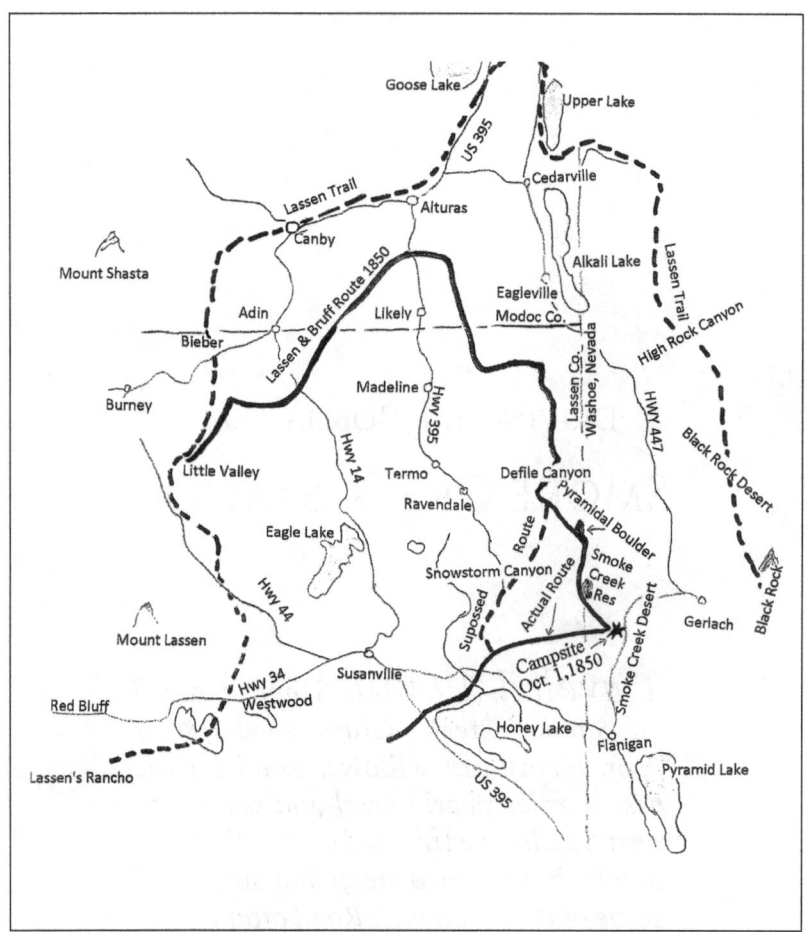

Updated Lord & Pratt map showing Lassen's and Bruff's actual route in 1850. (Original map on page 31)
Courtesy of Author

stopping place. A stage road from Susanville to Surprise Valley branched off the Nobles Road from here.

Because the citizens of the area needed protection from hostile Indians of the Honey Lake region, the site was sold in 1862 to the U.S. Army and was converted into a military

Nobles Emigrant Trail

camp. Twenty-five enlisted men of Company 2 California Volunteers, under the command of Lieutenant Henry W. Williams from Fort Crook, California, established their camp at Smoke Creek on December 15, 1862. The original fort was constructed of rock from the area. Desertion was rampant at the camp, so replacements were brought in every two to three weeks. Later, in October 1863, Nevada volunteers were ordered from Fort Churchill to replace the California troops and remained there until they were removed to Granite Creek Station in 1866.

When Captain Almond B. Wells arrived in June of 1864, he renamed the base Camp Pollock after Pennsylvania Governor James Pollock. Governor Pollock was famous at the time for coining the motto "In God We Trust" for the U. S. Mint.

A small graveyard contains the remains of: Pvt. John Smith, who died of "lead poisoning" after an altercation with an officer at Deep Hole Springs; Pvt. Gustav Platt, who died of typhoid; Sgt. Wm. McCoy, cause of death unknown; and Pvt. David O'Connell, who was killed in battle, allegedly with Indians.

William V. Kingsbury constructed a new trading post in the winter of 1862-1863, and soon thereafter he erected a hotel. He remained there in business for many years. Kingsbury adopted the name Smoke Creek Sam. He was elected to the Territorial Council for Roop County (later Washoe County) during that abortive attempt to attach this area to Nevada—an attempt that devolved from efforts of Isaac Roop, Peter Lassen, and other citizens of Susanville to establish the Nataqua Territory. The citizens of Honey Lake Valley didn't want to pay taxes to either California or to Nevada, so they tried to establish their own territory, which they called Nataqua. The Roop Post Office was active here from July 13, 1866 to August 6, 1867.

KEN JOHNSTON

Smoke Creek Station consisted of a large hotel and Smoke Creek Sam (William V. Kingsbury) stayed there until late in the 1860s. A typical example of his advertisement appeared in The Sage Brush printed January 12, 1867:

> WELL, WHILE YOU ARE ABOUT IT LOOK HERE!!
> The Celebrated Smoke Creek Station, situated on the Humboldt, Idaho, East Bannock, Reese River, Salt Lake, Surprise Valley, New York, London, Paris, Japan and China road, in fact from which point you can go anywhere if you want to, is still running, commanded by that well known individual, Smoke Creek Sam.[45]
>
> Owing to the immense travel to the above localities, we have made arrangements to accommodate it all, in a superior and gentlemanly like manner. We are endeavoring to induce the directors of the Pacific Railroad to locate the terminus of the road at Smoke Creek, it being we think, the most central point for it. San Francisco may "buck" a little against it, but geographical position will tell. It is unfortunate for San Francisco to be located so far away from Smoke Creek but we cant help it now. — Speaking of square meals, torch light processions, baled hay and "sich" like, there is where we understand ourselves. We can converse upon those subjects,

---
45 Amesbury p. 23 & 24.

NOBLES EMIGRANT TRAIL

in connection with that commercial article called cash, with the most perfect aplomb and nonchalance.

We most respectfully invite those going anywhere to call on us.
Kingsbury & Co.

Smoke Creek later became the private Smoke Creek Ranch of today. But before giving up the land, the Indians fought to retain it, and the area was defended by the formidable warrior, ironically also called Smoke Creek Sam.

Where the road turns west at the entrance to the ranch you can see the panorama Bruff sketched to the south. To the west, Rush Creek Canyon confluences with Smoke Creek, and the ruts of the Nobles Trail are very evident as they exit the valley.

Smoke Creek Ranch Road follows the Nobles Route here, avoiding the rugged Rush Creek Canyon just to the south. Before the road descends to the Rush Creek, the Trails West marker N-15 appears on the left. The trail crosses the road here and goes over a rise to the right, rather than dropping to the creek and Robbers Roost, as the current driving road does.

Swales going west out of Smoke Creek Meadow
north of Rush Creek canyon
Photo by Author

Nobles Emigrant Trail

Driving the Nobles Trail:
Robbers Roost

Robbers Roost is an impressive, steep-walled canyon of basaltic rock that makes a likely place for highwaymen. At least that was the thinking of the creative persons who named the canyon.

Information on the area is scarce, at best. According to Amesbury, the narrow defile was named because of "some formidable characters who had lived there a short time." History, though, is not generous in elaborating more on the name.

Rush Creek flows south from Rush Creek Mountain. It follows the California-Nevada state line, called Von Schmidt's 120th parallel (named after the surveyor who is credited with establishing the boundary).

Rush Creek continues through Robbers Roost as it drains the land to the west of Smoke Creek before the two creeks join.

Robbers Roost
Photo by Author

Nobles Trail swales descending from
Rush Creek Canyon bypass.
Photo by Author

Nobles Emigrant Trail

In spite of the forbidding name, Robbers Roost is a very inviting camping place, with cottonwood trees for shade and a burbling creek for ambiance.

As you leave Robbers Roost and continue west, you will cross the state line. Look back to see a good example of the Nobles Trail swale as it descends from the Rush Creek Bypass.

Continuing west, keep a wary eye open for the dinosaur that is reported to loom over the road and vehicles traveling it.

The road continues west over a flat plain where wild burros, pronghorns, coyotes, and other wildlife are often seen. When you pass Skedaddle Ranch Road watch the skyline to the west for the gunsight notch in the ridge above Mud Springs. To the south, the Skedaddle Mountains rise between Skedaddle Ranch and Honey Lake Valley beyond.

Dinosaur on Nobles Trail
Photo by Author

Gunsight Notch west of Mud Springs
Photo by Author

Nobles Emigrant Trail

Driving the Nobles Trail:
Mud Springs

Now known as Bull Creek Ranch and Bull Springs, it once sported a hotel called Mud Flat Station that provided a rest stop and supplies for travelers and their livestock.

In the fall of 1853, J. R. Bradway reported, "Good grass and tolerable water but not very plenty but little fuel." Others reported there was a good supply of water but little grass.

In 1861, Ruth Eliza Taylor wrote, "Came on ten miles to Mud Springs... At the springs we found another house, no roof, no windows. Here we bought one pound of butter and paid 75 cents for it; squash for 10 cents a pound."[46]

Today, the springs are used to water cattle in a peaceful setting, but they also had a violent history due to conflicts

---

46 Due to current inflation, that amount would add up to nearly $20, so prices were high.

Mud Springs today
Photo by Author

Skedaddle Mountains
Photo by Author

Nobles Emigrant Trail

between settlers and Native Americans who were trying to defend their homeland. Two such accounts follow

The first one, was told by A.L. Harper in *Fairfield's History of Lassen County*.

> ### Burning of the Mud Flat Station
>
> Along in December, 1861, Samuel Marriott started for the Humboldt with four or five ox teams loaded with freight. On the evening of their arrival at Rush creek they unyoked their cattle and drove them down on the flat below to feed. When they got back to the wagons they found some Indians plundering them, but they ran away as soon as they saw the teamsters coming. The next morning it was raining and snowing by spells and this weather continued for three or four days. When the storm was over the cattle were scattered and all of them could not be found, but Marriott used what he had, and by taking part of a load at a time, managed to get his freight back to the Mud Springs Station and store it in one of the buildings there.
>
> Hobbs, Robert Ross, and two men coming in from the Humboldt stayed there that winter. About the middle of March Hobbs came out to Honey Lake valley. Early one morning a few days after he had gone Ross heard the dog bark and a shot fired. An Indian had crawled up behind a bunch of willows

until he was only fifty or sixty yards from the house.

The dog discovered him, and not liking Indians, made an attack on him and the Indian had to shoot him in self defense. The bullet struck the dog back of the head and went the whole length of his body just under the skin. Ross thought that the Indians might be around and he jumped out of bed, grabbed his gun, and went out without putting on his clothes, for he wanted to get there before the Indian had time to reload his gun. The dog was still fighting the Indian and Ross got a shot at him.

He ran a little ways and then dropped his bow and arrows and a rabbit skin cloak. He succeeded in going a short distance further and there was met by two other Indians who helped him mount his horse. He hung to his gun and carried it away with him. The blood on the ground showed that he had been severely wounded.

In some way the Honey Lakers heard about the shooting of the Indian, and thinking there might be trouble about it, they hitched up five ox teams and went out there after Marriott's freight. When they got there they loaded it as rapidly as possible and left the place — the men who had been staying there going along with them. A night or two

NOBLES EMIGRANT TRAIL

afterwards the buildings at the station were all burned.

H. L. Spargur was coming in from the Humboldt and intended to stay there that night, but he saw the buildings burning and struck across the hills leaving the station to one side. This must have occurred during the first week of April.

A year later a second story of a violent conflict between settlers and Native Americans was reported by the *Quincy Union*.

MUD SPRINGS MASSACRE

The last of October 1862, a party started from the Humboldt mines to go to Honey Lake Valley. There were 11 men in all. Two of these men belonged in Honey Lake Valley and the rest of the party, so far as is known, were from Shasta County, and all were on their way to their homes. Some of them had business in the Humboldt mining towns and others were prospectors and teamsters. One man, Doby Dobyns, had a 4-horse team. Purdom and Kellogg, who were partners had another, and there was a lighter rig drawn by probably two horses. Stories are conflicting but the following is the truth in regard to the principal facts.

The Indians were troublesome, but large parties felt secure from attack.

KEN JOHNSTON

October 31, the party stayed at Smoke Creek. One of these men showed three Indian scalps said to be some of those taken from the Indians killed at Gravelly Ford the last of July, and said he wanted more of them.

He had a Sharps rifle and two revolvers and thought he could whip all the Indians they brought to him, and he wanted some brought. When the fight began, his horse ran away with him and so the red men escaped with their lives. The next morning, all the men except Green rolled their guns up in their blankets because they thought they were out of danger from an attack by the Indians. Green said he was going to stick to his gun and was ridiculed for his timidity.

When they came down off the bluffs onto the east end of Mud Flat about 9 miles from Shaffer's, a band of Indians estimated at from 15 to 50 rose up from behind some sagebrush that had piled up a short distance from the road and poured a volley into them. Purdom was shot just under the shoulder blade. It was a serious wound and he fell from the wagon. The horses then swung around and tipped the wagon over.

Green, Spencer, McCoy and another man were on horseback and a little distance ahead of the wagon, but the three immediately turned and rode back to them. In the fight that followed, Kellogg was shot through the heart and was killed instantly, McCoy was shot through the hip and Spencer was struck between the shoulders, almost on the neck, but either the bullet had no force or he had on a good many clothes, for it only raised a big lump. It is said that Block ran toward the Indians, some say making Masonic signs, others that he offered them money to spare his life, but they killed him before he got very far.

It was not much of a fight on the part of the whites and the man they laughed at that morning for his cowardice did most of the fighting. He fired at the Indians several times and killed one of them at least. He managed to keep them off until the other got into the light rig and drove off. Harper says they were going to leave Purdom on the ground, but Green made them go back and get him. McCoy's wound made it hard for him to remain on his horse and Green held him until they reached a safe place. The Indians pursued them for some distance, but they reached Shaffer's station in safety.

The dead men were left behind where they fell. The next day, five or six men took Shaffer's wagon and brought in the bodies of Kellogg and Block. The former

> was not mutilated but the last was cut up quite badly. Purdom and Kellogg's team had been taken away and the two wagons plundered. It was known that Block had $500 in money on him and the Indians got that. They took from Dobyn's wagon an express box containing some jewelry and considerable money, and from the other wagon, a sack in which was the money Purdom and Kellogg had received for their Humboldt mines. Mrs. M.J. McLear, who was Purdom's wife, said it was a goodly sum.
>
> Lomas and another man made some boxes and buried Kellogg and Block out in the sagebrush northwest of Shaffer's station. It was north of the road to Susanville and west of the Humboldt road, perhaps 20 or 30 rods from each of them. They were never moved from there. Purdom recovered to some extent, but two years later he died in San Francisco from effects of his wound. McCoy was crippled for life.[47]

This murder was also recorded in Fairfield's history as it caused great anger in the Honey Lake Valley, and a company was raised in Susanville to pursue the Indians. "It was thought by some that the attack on the whites at Mud Flat was made by Smoke Creek Sam's band. Others claimed that the Indians who made it had followed the party...and were taking revenge for the killing of Indians..."[48]

---

47 Fairfield. p. 294.
48 Ibid. p. 294.

NOBLES EMIGRANT TRAIL

Dreibelbis wrote that the Susan River was nine miles from Mud Springs and advised: "Emigrants should start early from Mud Springs as the road is covered with cobblestones which makes it slow and tedious. It is nearly level til you descend slightly to the valley of the stream (Honey Lake Valley). This is a delightful valley, its soil of the most productive kind, and is from 5-7 miles wide and covered in clover, blue joint, red top, and bunch grass in great abundance. The stream abounds in mountain trout which are easily taken with hook and line, and the wild rye hay grows as tall as a man on horseback."

As the road approaches Highway 395, it ascends a slope and parallels the Nobles Trail swale. You will pass the Trails West marker N-21 on the right.

When you get to the pavement, turn left on Highway 395, and in a short distance, you will come to the Nobles Emigrant Monument at View Land.

Trails West Marker N-21 Rocky ascent toward View Land
Photo by Author

Rocky swale toward Viewland
Photo by Author

Nobles Emigrant Trail

Driving the Nobles Trail:
View Land

The name is enticing. The area offers panoramic views of the Honey Lake, Honey Lake Valley, and the first sight of the Sierra Nevada for emigrants coming over the trail.

Bruff wrote that Lassen had been here earlier in the year and had discovered the lake, which Bruff called Derby Lake. He later learned that a member of Lassen's party had named it Honey Lake because of a "sweet dew" they obtained from grass growing in the area.

We now know that Lassen and Bruff had been as far east as Smoke Creek in 1850, and had probably followed this same route on their way to Honey Lake Valley.

The California State Park commission in cooperation with the Lassen County Historical Society placed a roadside marker on August 15, 1959. A base was built and the plaque

KEN JOHNSTON

Nobles Emigrant Trail monument at View Land
Photo by Author

Nobles Emigrant Trail

was remounted on May 4, 1985 by the Neversweats Chapter No. 1863 E Clampus Vitus. It reads:

> NOBLE EMIGRANT TRAIL
> THE ROUTE WAS FIRST USED IN 1852 BY EMIGRANTS TO NORTHERN CALIFORNIA SEEKING TO AVOID THE HARDSHIPS OF THE LASSEN TRAIL. IT CROSSED THE DESERT FROM THE HUMBOLDT RIVER IN NEVADA, PASSED THIS POINT, AND PROCEEDED OVER THE MOUNTAINS TO THE TOWN OF SHASTA. LATER, 1859-1861, IT WAS KNOWN AS THE FT. KEARNY, SOUTH PASS AND HONEY LAKE WAGON ROAD. FROM THIS POINT PETER LASSEN AND J.G. BRUFF ON OCTOBER 4, 1850, SAW HONEY LAKE WHILE ON AN EXPEDITION HUNTING FOR GOLD LAKE.

Hutchings California Magazine published a picture of the lake, valley, and mountains in an article written by John A. Dreibelbis in its June 1857 issue.

The original title to Nobles Pass referred to the route from here, along the Susan River to where the trail joined the Lassen Trail east of Mount Lassen. The route around the mountain that he apparently was shown by Lassen didn't become called Nobles Pass until later.

View Land gave Lassen and Bruff and later travelers on the Nobles Trail their first views of Honey Lake and its rich valley.

KEN JOHNSTON

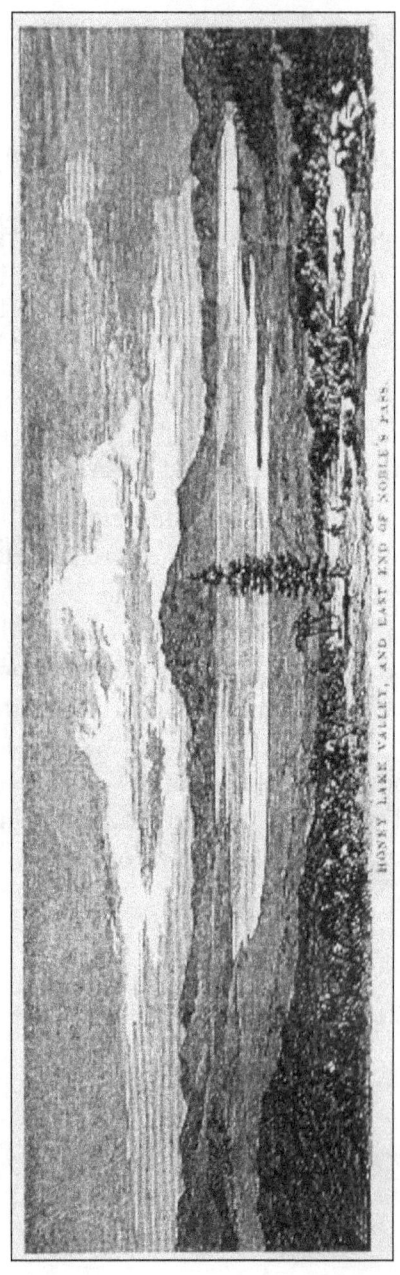

Honey Lake drawing in June 1857 *Hutchings California Magazine.*

Nobles Emigrant Trail

Driving the Nobles Trail:
Shaffer Station

From View Land, the trail dropped down to Shaffer Station, where a trading post was established. Benjamin Ruggles stopped at the station in 1859 and recorded in his journal: "Here we find feed and water good...We see here the first newspapers we have seen for a long time. Begin to think we are approaching civilication [sic]. Feel pretty well over it." His quote is on the Trails West, Inc. marker N-23 by the coral just south of the highway.

Shortly beyond the station and just south of the town of Litchfield, the trail crossed the Susan River at Soldier's Bridge. The bridge was built in the summer of 1860 by First Lieutenant Hamilton and his soldiers. They arrived in Honey Lake Valley at the request of local citizens following many conflicts with Indians and finally the murder of Horace Adams on June 18, 1860.

Trails West marker N-23 Shaffer Station
Photo by Author

Shaffer Station later called Mapes Ranch.
Shaffer Mountain stands behind.
Photo by Author

Nobles Emigrant Trail

The soldiers established Camp Honey Lake here. They built a structure to house the soldiers and a corral for the horses. A post office later operated here from 1864 to 1867.

The trail followed the Susan River from the bridge to Susanville. Several emigrants traveling this section in the 1850s commented on Indian attacks and depredations. Randal, in 1852 wrote, "This morning our neighbor campers found one of their oxen shot by the Indians; nearly dead. The ox had 5 arrows sticking in him from 2 to 10 inches deep; the Indians have not showed themselves today."

Soldier's Bridge over Susan River.
Photo by Author

Mary Fish wrote in 1860, "The Indians have been troublesome here last spring they murdered several of the inhabitants & committed numerous depredations."

In 1860, Allen Tyrell was following the river to

KEN JOHNSTON

Susanville. Near where Willow Creek flows into it, he recorded: "... a fine clear stream and larger than that Susan river is here. It is said that a man named Nobles explored this section of country at an early day and that his wife was drowned in the stream by which we are camped and has taken her name." (Note, Susan River was indeed named by Nobles in honor of his wife, who had remained in Minnesota, and her drowning here could only be hearsay or imagined as an "alternate fact.")

Nobles Emigrant Trail

Driving the Nobles Trail:
Roop Town – Susanville

Isaac Roop was among the group from Shasta City to accompany Nobles to verify his claims about the route to the Humboldt. Roop was impressed with the Honey Lake area and its potential, and when a fire in June of 1853 destroyed his business in Shasta City, he came to the Honey Lake Valley where he claimed the land that would become Susanville. He then went back to Shasta City, but returned to his claim with merchandise and supplies in 1854 and 1855.

Roop built a log cabin that became his trading post, also known as Roop's Fort. The settlement that built up around the fort was known as Rooptown. The name was changed to Susanville in 1857 to honor Isaac Roop's daughter, Susan.

Also in 1855, Peter Lassen returned to the valley prospecting for gold. He found a small gold claim, and built a cabin. In 1856, word got out about his discovery, and miners flocked into the area.

KEN JOHNSTON

Roop's Fort and Isaac Roop.   *Photo by Robert Amesbury*

Susanville became the center of activity for the Honey Lake Valley. The valley's rich, fertile soil and fresh water supplied by mountain streams made it attractive to settlers. Winters were mild enough livestock didn't need to be supplemented with much hay, and hay could be cut from wild bunch grass that grew in abundance. Crops of grains, fruits, and vegetables could be raised by irrigation, and wildlife was plentiful for hunting.

Life was good, indeed so good in the valley that *The Humboldt Register* of April 30, 1864 published:

Ode to Indolence, the Never Sweats

"That is the trite sobriquet given here to the people of Honey Lake valley. It is so easy to get a living there, that people acquire indolent habits, we suppose." Well, that will do to introduce our anecdote, anyhow. A man advertised for three able-bodied men.

People who advertise get everything they want and in a few days three men—stout fellows—came

Nobles Emigrant Trail

in company and applied for the place. 'Ready to commence tomorrow?' he asked. 'Yes,' said the spokesman of the trio. 'O, I forgot! Where have you come from?' 'From Honey Lake,' they replied. 'Honey Lake be d....d' said he as he walked off, 'What do you suppose I want? I want men to work. Honey Lake,' and he would not hear another word."[49]

Roop's Fort, which stands next to the Lassen Historical Museum, has recently been renovated. In the city park below the fort and museum stands the stone and brass monument stating: "This meadow, now a city park, was a welcome stopping place on the Noble Emigrant Trail, pioneered by William H. Nobles in 1851 and first used in 1852. Here, emigrants en route to the Northern California mines were able to rest, recruit their stock, and obtain needed provisions at Isaac Roop's establishment, from which grew the City of Susanville."

Nobles Emigrant Trail plaque in Susanville city park.
Photo by Author

---

49 Fairfield, p. 363

KEN JOHNSTON

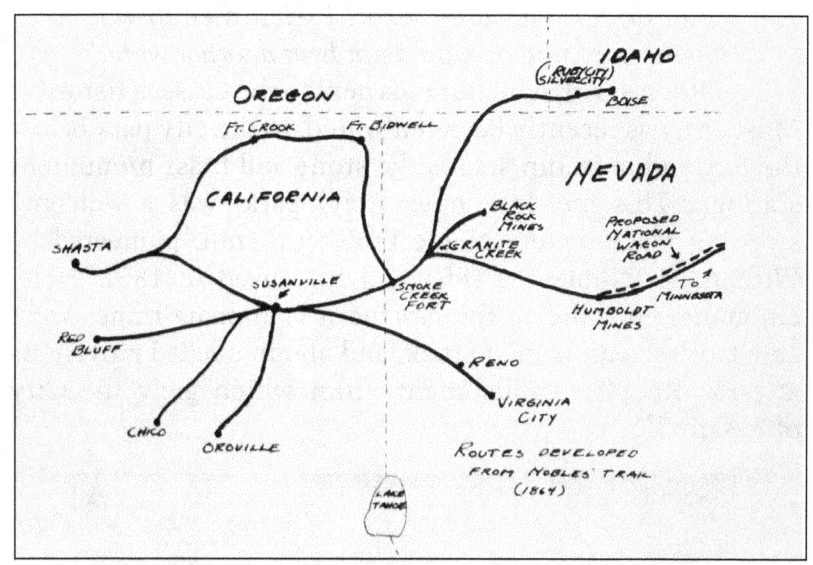

Map by Robert Amesbury showing roads
utilizing the Nobles Route.

NOBLES EMIGRANT TRAIL

OVERLAND AND IDAHO ROUTES

With California becoming a state in 1850, there continued to be a large influx of people. In the late 1850s and early 1860s, Susanville became a crossroads of travel connecting Marysville, Chico, and Shasta City in the Sacramento Valley with mining areas in Idaho, the Black Rock area, and the Comstock Lode in Nevada City.

Some of the people settled in the Honey Lake Valley, as it was the first place emigrants from the East could find supplies, good feed for their livestock, and could rest. It is said that the wild rye grass grew as tall as a man on horseback, and that it originally covered much of the valley.

The Comstock silver strikes in 1859 created a prosperous market for livestock and produce from the Honey Lake area. Also, with gold and silver strikes in Ruby City and Silver City in Idaho, the people of Susanville realized the advantage of establishing a road here.

In 1863 a toll road was developed to run from Chico

KEN JOHNSTON

to Honey Lake. From Susanville, the route then followed the Nobles Trail east to Granite Creek and turned north through Soldier Meadows and Summit Lake toward Ruby City.

Robert Amesbury, in his book, *Nobles' Emigrant Trail*, quoted an article from the *Sage Brush* newspaper saying: "We must pause in our account of the discovery of the Black Rock mines, in order to give some account of the town of Susanville—a town which, by reason of these discoveries, and its situation on the great thoroughfare leading from California to Black Rock, Idaho, Montana, and Humboldt, bids fair to become, next to San Francisco, the most important town on the Pacific Coast."

Note: The following four pages are taken from Amesbury's rendition of a section of Fairfield's History of Lassen County:

THE OVERLAND AND IDAHO ROUTES

When the Idaho mining excitement broke out in 1862, the people of this section realized the advantage of establishing a route for the transportation of passengers and goods to the new mines by way of the Nobles' pass and began to take steps to secure such a route. By the act of April 14, 1863, the legislature granted a franchise to John C. Bidwell, J.C. Mandeville, R.M. Cochran and John Guill, to construct a toll road from Chico to Honey Lake. They incorporated the following year as the Chico and Humboldt Wagon Road Company, and completed their road to Susanville.

Early in the spring of 1865, parties went from Susanville to Ruby City and return, going

Nobles Emigrant Trail

by way of Shaeffer's, Mud Springs, Deep Hole, Granite Creek, Soldier Meadows, Summit Lake, Mint Springs, Gridley Springs, Pueblo, Trout Creek, Willow Creek, White Horse Creek, Crooked River, Castle Creek, Owyhee River, Jordan Creek Valley and Wagontown to Ruby City a distance of 332 miles.

The same spring Pierce & Francis, backed by General Bidwell, started weekly saddle-train from Chico to Idaho, by this route, to carry passengers and mail. ("The Grizzly Bear" of April, 1915, says: "The first saddle train from Chico to Idaho, via Susanville, left Chico on April 3rd [1865] in command of Captain Pierce, an old pioneer of the mountains of the Pacific Coast. Passengers riding on the hurricane deck of a mule paid a fare of $66. This included the use of a roll of blankets to sleep under and the carrying of a supply of provisions. There were forty passengers in the first saddle train.")

Later in the year Major John Mullen became manager of the enterprise. Several stages were constructed, the route was stocked, and on July 11, 1865, the first stage from Chico to Ruby City passed through Susanville. I. N. Roop was advisory agent of the line, and W. N. DeHaven local agent. This trip occupied sixteen days, because of the newness of the road and the hostility of the Indians.

This latter difficulty was so exaggerated by the newspapers that the new route met with but little favor from the traveling public. The discovery of the Black Rock mines about

Freighting to the Humboldt
Photo Robert Amesbury

Stage to Silver City
Photo from Robert Amesbury

Nobles Emigrant Trail

this time (their first discovery was in 1849), and the great rush to that region, also increased the importance of the Susanville Route. In May, 1866, the *Sage Brush* stated:

"The immigration to Idaho and Montana has commenced. Every day trains of men, mules, horses, and sometimes jackasses, pass through our town on a weary pilgrimage to the distant mining camps...

"In May, also, the California and Idaho Stage and Fast Freight Company was incorporated, with a capital stock of $200,000. John Mullen was president. About midnight, July 1, 1866, the first stage left Chico, and arrived in Ruby City in three days and five hours, a distance of 427 miles. Susanville soon acquired considerable importance as a staging center. Eight stages per week arrived there from Chico, Red Bluff, Oroville, Virginia City, and other points.

"The reports of the fabulous richness of the Black Rock and Owyhee mines drew a constant stream of travel through this section, and it was necessary to increase the facilities of the stage line. This was done, a daily stage was put on, and James D. Byers was appointed general superintendent of the line. They ran daily till winter set in, and then the deep snows so interferred that only about two trips a week could be made.

KEN JOHNSTON

> "When the contract expired the next year, the Central Pacific had completed its track east of the Sierra nearly to the big bend of the Humboldt, reducing the distance to be staged by one-half. For this reason, the government refused to renew the mail contract, freight and travel were diverted to the new route, and Susanville was compelled to relinquish its dream of rivaling San Francisco in wealth and importance."

From Susanville to Shasta City only parts of this portion of the trail were used to any extent since the complete road itself, running as it did around the northern edge of Lassen Peak, was closed large parts of the year by snow, and secondly there did not develop the hoped-for traffic between Shasta and Susanville by this route. [50]

Author's note: thus ends Amesbury quote.

---

50 Amesbury pp. 29-31.

Nobles Emigrant Trail

Big Spring

In leaving Susanville, the trail turned north and commenced its ascent of the mountains, then shortly turned west following a heavily timbered and stony ridge. In a little over a couple miles, the road forked at a point where Trails West has placed one of its rail markers (N-27), which quotes Mary C. Fish's September 12, 1860 journal entry, "We commenced the assent directly on leaving the city...the greater portion of the company took the road to Marysville while the remaining portion & ourselves included have taken the Red Bluff Road."

It was at this point that the Humbug Road from Marysville joined the Nobles Trail. It was completed in 1857. At this point travelers could choose to go that way, following the trail to the left, or continue on to the right on the Nobles Trail and come to Big Spring, where they found "a large spring of the finest water."

Isaac Roop made improvements to the spring, and today it has been enlarged to supply water to sprinkle logging roads to keep down dust.

Pond below Big Spring
Photo by Author

Nobles Emigrant Trail

Nobles Pass

From Big Spring, the trail turned more northerly and continued west over heavily timbered flat terrain past what is now Hog Flat Reservoir. It then angled north around a small butte and essentially followed the modern graveled Bridge Creek Spring Road as it crossed Nobles Pass.

A Trails West marker N-29 has Benjamin Ruggles Aug. 13, 1859 quote: "We have risen to a considerable height today, though our road has been 'up and down.' We are now crossing the Sierra Nevada Mountains by 'Nobles Pass' said to be the easiest pass of three."

The pass is so named because it is a divide where water flowing east joins the Susan River (named by Nobles to honor his wife) and flows into the endorheic basin of Honey Lake east of the mountains. Water flowing to the west merges with other streams flowing into the Sacramento Valley. Thus, as John Dreibelbis wrote in his 1853 waybill,

Trails West Marker N-29 for Nobles Pass
Photo by Author

Nobles Emigrant Trail

the summit was "impossible to ascertain the precise place, owing to the flatness of the country."

Continuing northwesterly, the trail follows Bridge Creek and passes through a meadow along the creek that became a favorite emigrant camping area.

Trails West marker N-30 states: "This is a fine valley and has the purest and coldest water a man ever drank...I think this the most pleasant camping place we have had, fine pine timbers...found the grave of Nancy Allen today."— Gorham Gates Kimball, Jun 23, 1865.

The grave is in a fenced enclosure in the meadow and has other signage telling the story of "some poor emigrant woman" who died on her way to California.

From the Allen grave, the trail goes southwest, following Bridge Creek for about a mile then continues west to Feather Lake.

Nancy Ann Allen Gravesite
Photo by Author

KEN JOHNSTON

It was at Feather Lake where Nobles intersected the Lassen Trail as he explored the route in 1850. It was here that he apparently realized the importance of his discovery of Nobles Pass just to the east, and how it could provide an easy cutoff to the Lassen Route, as he then followed the already established Lassen Trail into the Sacramento Valley and Lassen's Rancho.

There is little recorded information as to how much previous contact Nobles had had with Lassen other than what "old settlers in Honey Lake Valley claimed" that Lassen had known the route "before Mr. Noble ever saw it" and had been his guide.

But when Nobles arrived at Lassen's Ranch at *Bosquejo*, Lassen was not there. So he continued on to Yerba Buena (later San Francisco) where he met Lassen at Henry Gerke's house with his proposal to establish ranches along his route, with Lassen's being the last ranch at the entrance to the Sacramento Valley.

Trails West Feather Lake Marker L-32.
Photo by Author

NOBLES EMIGRANT TRAIL

Feather Lake
Photo by Author

After this meeting, they returned to Lassen's Ranch. Nobles went with Lassen back to Feather Lake and explored a new route around the north side of Mount Lassen over terrain that Lassen had previously been over in 1846 and in 1850.

From Feather Lake, the Nobles Trail then followed the Lassen Trail northwest to Pine Creek where there was good water and plenty of grass. Legend has it that people going south on the Lassen Trail to Sacramento Valley would pass people going north on the Nobles Trail to Sacramento Valley! Each would learn from the other that they were going opposite directions to the same destination.

At Pine Creek Valley, emigrants following the Nobles Trail found plenty of water and grass. In 1860, Mary C. Fish wrote, "The timber here grows to an amazing size there being timber enough to supply the continent of America: There is

Pine Creek Valley, showing easy route over the mountains.
Photo by Author

Poison Lake
Photo by Author

Nobles Emigrant Trail

also plenty of game consisting of Grizzly Bears, Mountain Sheep, Deer, Foxes, &c. I saw the track of a Grizzly Bear which being measured by one of the company was found to be eight inches long & six inches in diameter." Note: There are no longer grizzlies or mountain sheep in the area, but recently wolves and wolf tracks have been seen.

At the west end of Pine Creek Valley, Nobles Trail branched to the west from the Lassen Trail and continued through Dry Valley to Poison Lake. The lake gets its name from a historic legend that tells of small red spiders that lived on the surface. The bites of these spiders would cause a red rash to develop on areas that were washed with the water. It is said that the native people living in the Poison Lake area, being immune to the bites, joked that whites—in order to keep from developing the rash—had to bathe with their clothes on!

KEN JOHNSTON

Nobles Emigrant Trail

Butte Creek to Sunflower Flat and Manzanita Lake

The trail continued west of Poison Lake to Butte Creek Meadows, where there was good camping, plenty of water and grass. But there were also Indian dangers, as Solomon Kingery reported on August 15, 1852:

> The Indians Shot 7 oxen for the company last night again. Only one died; then to day Som of our Company layed in the Bush after the teams left to watch the Indians. After awhile one come up the Creek looking and watching on every side. When he got within about 100 yards he heard or Seen the boys. He started to run. Seven of the

boys Shot at him. They wounded him. They followed him about one mile; he was still running. They could easily track him by the blood. We think he bled to death.

The original trail in 1852 followed south up Butte Creek, which the emigrants called Black Butte Creek to (Black) Butte Lake via Bath Tub Lake. "Here," according to Amesbury, "lacking an axe to blaze the trail, trees along the way were bent at the tip to point the way. Some of these within the park boundaries have evaded the hungry saws of loggers and may still be plainly seen around Bath Tub Lake."

Butte Creek with Lassen Park mountains in background.
Photo by Author

Rangers and tourists still bathe in Bath Tub Lake. Legend has it that an emigrant on the trail, having crossed the dusty desert, stopped here, and when he bathed, he washed off so much dirt that he claimed he found a pair of shorts he thought he'd lost a couple weeks before.

Nobles Emigrant Trail

Black Butte to Hat Creek

From Bath Tub Lake the trail passed by the north shore of Butte Lake and continued along the present trail to the Cinder Cone (Black Butte), passing between it and Prospect Peak to the north. Here the trail continued on past Soap Lake and Emigrant Lake and crossed Badger Flat over an area covered with black volcanic ash, which hooves and wheels sank into several inches. The trail followed the Lassen Volcanic National Park boundary just inside the Park, then crossed Hat Creek at Emigrant Ford just outside the Park before turning back into the Park and heading on toward Lassen Peak. This place was later covered by the Devastated Area, which resulted from the 1915 Mount Lassen eruption.

After fording Hat Creek, the trail turned southwest for about a half mile and crossed Lost Creek. Continuing southwest, it re-entered the Park and crossed Highway 89 near the Chaos Crags Group Campground. It then climbed up a fairly steep slope to Sunflower Flat, where the Park has a bronze plaque and an interpretive panel about Nobles Trail.

Nobles Trail by Cinder Cone in Lassen Volcanic National Park
Photo by Author

Sunflower Flat in Lassen Volcanic National Park
Photo by Author

Nobles Emigrant Trail

At one time the author enacted a living history program with horses, oxen, and a covered wagon while he was a Lassen Park ranger/interpreter stationed there. Later the program and wagon were moved to the Manzanita Lake area.

Author and ox team at Sunflower Flat on Nobles Emigrant Trail
Photo Courtesy of Author

Going west from Sunflower Flat, the trail went through a heavily forested area. It then continued on to the Chaos Jumbles and Old Summertown, where seasonal rangers were housed. It passed Reflection Lake and Manzanita Lake, and the north entrance to the Park. It is here where campgrounds and a concession store with supplies and gasoline are available. The district ranger station and the Loomis Museum are also located here.

Nobles Emigrant Trail from Sunflower Flat
through Lassen Volcanic National Park
Photo by Author

Nobles Emigrant Trail

Benjamin Franklin Loomis, known as Frank, arrived at Manzanita Lake in 1874, built a cabin and also established Viola farther down the Nobles Trail. Loomis became a skilled photographer who documented the volcanic eruptions of Lassen Peak from 1914 to 1921 and the resultant devastation and mudflows that inundated part of the Nobles Trail along Hat Creek and Lost Creek in the Park. He was instrumental in the establishment of Lassen Volcanic National Park in 1916. He built the Loomis Museum and Visitor Center in 1927. Later, he and his wife, Estella, donated the museum and forty acres to the Park.

Loomis Museum and Visitor Center,
Lassen Volcanic National Park
Photo by Author

KEN JOHNSTON

> *In 1914...I climbed to the top of Lassen Peak six times...taking pictures...I realized that if the mountain should blow off while I was looking into...the crater, I would not be here to tell the tale. But for all that I never experienced the feeling of fear. For I was there to take pictures, and the pictures were the principal object of my thought.*
> B.F. Loomis

Just west of the Old Summertown and Manzanita Lake area the Nobles Trail of 1852-1854 joins the Nobles Trail of 1855 and later, which comes down from Eskimo Hill to the north. From here, the trail continued west through the Manzanita Chute and paralleled Highway 44 west to Deer Flat.

Nobles Emigrant Trail

Butte Creek West to Hat Creek: An Alternate Route

Originally called Poinsett Creek, Hat Creek was re-named by surveyor Drury D. Harrill in 1852. While traveling with the Nobles Party, he lost his prized hat when his horse stumbled on a rock while crossing it. He was unable to recover the hat, and he had to go bare-headed for the rest of the trip.

After 1855, an alternative route for the Nobles Trail traveled west from Butte Creek Meadows. It was made possible by the opening of the Lockhart Road that was established by Sam and Harry Lockhart that year, to carry freight from Red Bluff to Yreka. They found a serviceable route over the Hat Creek Rim, which had been a major barrier to wagons from Peter Lassen's attempt in 1848 until the Lockhart brothers found a way down the steep descent

Summit Lake
Photo by Author

Summit Juniper
Photo by Author

Nobles Emigrant Trail

in 1855. Called Hat Creek Hill by the emigrants, it was steep and at the bottom it crossed the volcanic landscape of Devil's Half Acre.

After its discovery, most traffic on Nobles Trail went west from Butte Creek Meadows on the Lockhart Road, following the route of modern Highway 44 past the nearly dry Summit Lake to Hat Creek Rim. About five miles west of Butte Creek the trail passed Summit Lake.

Emigrants or wagon drovers may have stopped in the shade of the Summit Juniper. It still stands between the modern highway and the lake, and an interpretive sign states that it is seven feet and seven inches in diameter, twenty-three feet and five inches in circumference, fifty-one feet tall. Its age is estimated to be approximately 515 years.

When the Nobles Trail came by here in the 1850s, the Summit Juniper would have been approximately 350 years old—a large tree at the time. When the emigrants passed, they may have rested under it. Also, there is a Trails West marker, N-38, near the tree that is inscribed:

NOBLES TRAIL—SNOW CAPPED MOUNTAINS.
THERE HAS BEEN SNOW CAPPED
MOUNTAINS IN SIGHT FOR THE LAST
WEEK. THIS EVENING SHASTA PEAK,
LAWSONS BUTTE ARE IN PLAIN VIEW &
THEY RESEMBLE LARGE BANKS OF SNOW.
— MARY C. FISH, SEP. 14, 1860.

This alternate route of the Nobles Trail was lower in elevation, had less snow in winter, and it avoided the soft volcanic ash near the Black Butte (Cinder Cone).

In crossing this area on June 19, 1865, Gorham Gates Kimball wrote:

KEN JOHNSTON

> The road through here was always a problem...George and myself rode on to top of Hat Creek Hill to prospect road, found a very high and rockey mountain we have to go up. Shall have to pack our load up as it will be all horses can do to get the waggon up - fine grass and water here. Found the graves of two white men killed by the Indians - poor fellows died in a very wild and heartless place. Passed over the Devil's half acre today and it is well named - it is about 4 miles of Burnt Rocks as thick as they can lay on top of each other.

On June 20 he wrote:

> Drove 8 miles to a small valley east of Lawson' Butte, came over the Devil's ½ Acre, it is about 3 miles of rocks, no soil. About half way over we found where the rocks all came from. It has been a volcanic eruption. The mouth or crater is a hole about 70 ft. long, 40 ft. wide, and about 20 ft. deep, with a natural bridge over the center about 6 ft. wide splendidly arched. The face of the country around appears to of been burnt by an immense fire – is truly a great curiosity. Next came Hat Creek Hill about 1 mile long and nearly perpendicular, same kind of rocks. The Devil truly was liberal of his rocks or his sack bursted and he spilled what he had...broke camp about 4

Nobles Emigrant Trail

o'clock this morning. All went back, unloaded the wagon, packed 4 of the horses with about 150# each took that up, came back, then I put a rope to the end of the pole and to the horn of my saddle, so with "Black Bird's" help the team made it. This is a big barren looking country, do not see what Providence make it for – think he set fire to it after he got it done, but the fire must of went out, so now he has no account of it in his books.

From the Old Station area, the trail followed up Hat Creek, over Eskimo Hill, and west of Table Mountain to join the older route west of Manzanita Lake.

KEN JOHNSTON

Nobles Emigrant Trail

Wells Fargo Gold a Mystery?

Traveling up Hat Creek Canyon today, the lure of gold legends can sound the siren call to search for the stash of stolen Wells Fargo gold said to be hidden somewhere in Hat Creek Canyon.

> *A Wells Fargo stage was held up between Anderson and Cottonwood and $40,000 in gold pieces and other coins were stolen by three armed bandits. Captain Schuler [from Foot of the Mountain Station] and his home guards followed the robbers up the ridge of Hat Creek in Mount Lassen's rugged terrain.*
>
> *The robbers hid there trying to escape and dug holes in which to hold water. In the exchange of gun fire Schuler and*

his men killed two of the robbers and wounded a third, who offered to show them where the money was hidden. He told them the money was buried in Hat Creek canyon under a rocky bluff but he died before he could show the exact location where the money was hidden. Treasure seekers have searched the area in vain for many years but so far as known the stolen money has never been recovered.[51]

Others think the bandits hid the money close to the scene of the robbery, hoping to make their escape, unburdened, and later return to get it. Where the scene of the robbery was, is hard to determine!

---
51 Schuler, p. 28.

Nobles Emigrant Trail

Manzanita Chute to Battle Creek

Manzanita Chute leads west from the junction of the two Nobles routes near Manzanita Lake and gets its name from the dense growth of "Rassberry" bushes as mentioned by Solomon Kingery. "Road very hard to Brake on account of Stone and Chaperal Brush. Encamped on Rassberry Creek [now called Manzanita Creek]. Grass rather (poor) but abundanc of Mt. Rassberrys. Here we enjoyed the after noon by picking and Eating them. They are a very good berry." The "Chaperal Brush" and "Rassberrys" he refers to are the Manzanita bushes, with berries that tend to be very tart.

In this area, there must have been some rather magnificent trees, as reported in a couple journal entries. Tosten Kittelsen Stabaek in 1852 wrote, "On the descent we found many large trees; one that we measured had a circumference of twenty feet." And J. D. Randal measured one at twenty-two feet in circumference the same year.

KEN JOHNSTON

VIOLA RESORT

In addition to their home at Manzanita Lake, Frank Loomis homesteaded Viola in 1888 and named it after his mother. He worked as a shakemaker, and he purchased a mill and operated a store at the site. He freighted his shakes to the valley and hauled freight back to Shingletown on his return trips. In 1923, Loomis purchased the Shingletown Hotel, a two-story wooden structure with approximately twelve rooms. He later moved it to Viola, and established it as the Viola Resort. In 1905, it was destroyed by fire and replaced with a larger building in almost the same place. Sadly though, in 1953, it too was destroyed by fire. Even more sad, Mrs. Loomis died in Anderson of natural causes on the same day it burned."[52]

---

52 Smith, Dottie. "Travelin' In Time," March 12, 2010.

NOBLES EMIGRANT TRAIL

DEER FLAT

Deer Flat was the first meadow that provided feed and a good camping area after Butte Creek Meadows, and many emigrants stopped there. Brock and Black, in *A Guide To Nobles Trail*, state that:

> Soon after the Nobles Trail was opened, enterprising traders established ranches that served as trading posts and stopping places for emigrants heading to the upper Sacramento Valley. Emigrant diarists often mention them. Among the earliest was John Hill's [established in 1852]. As the years passed, these ranches and trading posts frequently exchanged ownership, with some developing into inns, hotels, and station stops for freighting and stage operations."

KEN JOHNSTON

Deer Flat
Photo by Author

NOBLES EMIGRANT TRAIL

In *Dictionary of Early Shasta County History*, Dottie Smith writes that Hill's Trading Post, aka Old Hill Station, was "Established in 1852 by John Hill on the south side of Deer Flat beside Nobles Emigrant Trail. It became a popular roadhouse and stopping place and eventually became known as Deer Flat."

John Dreibelbis's report places John Hill's Ranch at Deer Flat, but John S. L. Taylor wrote in 1854, that they camped at Jack Hill's ranch on Battle Creek. Brock and Black, also referring to Battle Creek, wrote that, "Due to its flat ground and extensive meadows, this camping area was heavily used by the emigrants traveling the Nobles Trail. Many emigrants paused here to recruit their livestock at Hill's Ranch/Trading Post in 1854 and at Brand and LaTour's Ranch/Trading Post in 1859 and later."

Amesbury also indicated Deer Flat was the location of Hill's ranch when he wrote, "This was one of the meadows seeded by the U. S. Government in early days as they were doing for many meadows in this area since a real migration of settlers to this area was expected."

Amesbury added:

> From here the trail went to Mountain Home along a present road (already in existence). This is where John Hill's trading post (mentioned by Dreibelbiss) was located probably about 1 year after this Noble Pass was opened. It then went southwest some 8 miles to McCumbers mill on Mill Creek. Before reaching McCumbers mill it had to cross Battle Creek. Now this original crossing shows how little this country had been scouted even though McCumber mill

was the first white settlement Nobles contacted. A short two miles up Battle Creek from the Nobles crossing was a much easier crossing. This crossing was soon discovered and used later, but this work deals with the original road.[53]

The actual location of John Hill's Ranch is not known. Several descriptions say either Deer Flat or on Battle Creek. Asa Fairfield wrote, "...to John Hill's ranch on Deer Flat on the north fork of Battle creek."[54] Perhaps Deer Flat, at that time, extended to Battle Creek.

BATTLE CREEK AND McCUMBER RESERVOIR

Trails West marker N-52 stands close to the dam on McCumber Reservoir. The trail went through the meadow that is now covered with water. The dam was built in 1906 and covered the meadow on Battle Creek where George McCumber moved when he sold his mill on Millseat Creek in 1850. After his death the property later came under the ownership of the Northern Power Company, which built the dam.

---

53 Amesbury p.33
54 Fairfield's *History of Lassen County*, p. 19

Nobles Emigrant Trail

Big Wheels

The Big Wheels Restaurant and Bar, named for the logging big wheels that had stood on the site, used to be one of the great watering holes in Shasta County, known far and wide for Leonard's famous Bloody Marys. The restaurant burned to the ground twice in recent years. A massive stone fireplace is all that remains.

Big Wheels used to haul logs near Shingletown
Photo by Author

Harriet Ball grave in Ogburn Cemetery
Photo by Author

Nobles Emigrant Trail

Ball Mill

Across the highway for Big Wheels is the location of the Ball Mill, built by W.W. Ball on Mill Creek. His wife, Harriet Ball died in 1860 and was buried in the Ogburn Cemetery west of Shingletown. Her grave marker has the oldest date in the graveyard.

Ball later sold the mill and bought Ball Ferry across the Sacramento River. Ball purchased the ferry from Pierson B. Reading. The ferry was initially a log embarkation point for sending logs to Sutter's Fort. It was later replaced by a bridge, but it still serves as a boat launching site on the river. It was dedicated in 1972 as a State of California Point of Historical Interest.

KEN JOHNSTON

Nobles Emigrant Trail

Shingletown

Originally called Shingle Camp, Shingletown was established to provide shingles and shakes. It was located where several roads from logging and mill sites converged. "James King and Thomas Asbury were possibly the first shingle- and shake-makers. In 1850, they set up camp and established their lucrative business beside Shingle Creek."[55]

Shingletown was originally a small village with a blacksmith shop, and a large barn for freight teams used to haul merchandise, plus shingles and shakes, to and from the valley. There was also a small dry goods store that sold textiles, clothing, boots, and supplies to loggers and travelers.

A saloon in the back of the store was apparently the local hangout. On September 15, 1860, Allen Tyrell wrote, "There was a fine little tavern here besides a blacksmith shop and dwelling houses. A shooting match came off after we arrived." On the following day he wrote, "...and gamblers

---
55   Smith, Dottie. "Travelin' In Time."

are playing cards in the tavern. They spent the whole of last night gambling."

The first Shingletown Store was built by John Freeland in 1854. In 1871, Freeland sold to John McCarley, who made improvements and took in Albert Smith as a partner and established the McCarley and Smith General Merchandise, Trading Post and Hotel. Their business became a very popular place. This store was a short distance from today's Shingletown Store. It was demolished in 1966.[56]

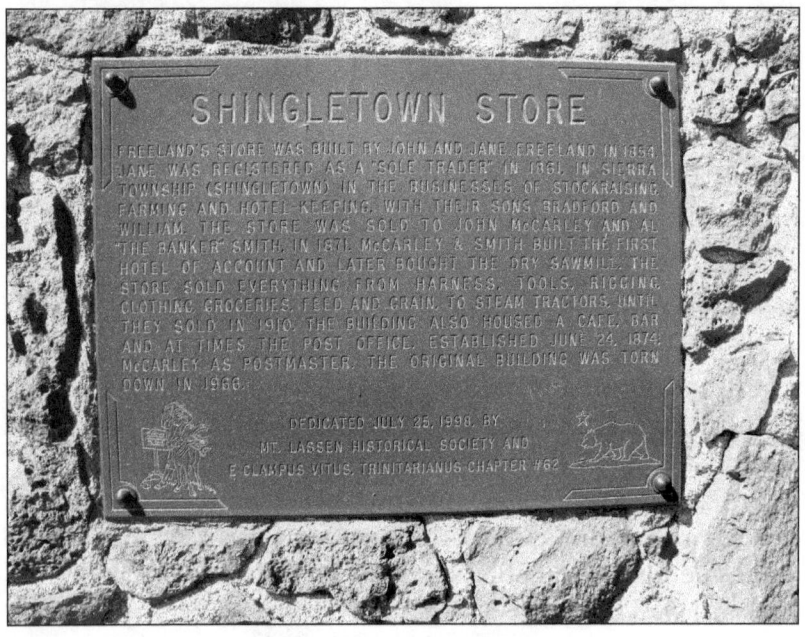

Shingletown Store plaque
Photo by Author

---

56   ibid.

Nobles Emigrant Trail

Making shingles in Shingletown
Courtesy of Shasta Historical Society

Trails West marker N-55 Shingletown
Photo by Author

Trails West marker N-56 Charley's Ranch
Photo by Author

Nobles Emigrant Trail

Charlie's Ranch (aka Charley's Ranch)

Trails West Marker N-56, "Nobles Trail - Charley's Ranch," is located just a few yards beyond a gate. If the ranch is running cattle, the gate may be closed. If so, park and walk through. Please keep the gate closed.

Charles (Charley or Charlie) Ogburn established his homestead with a large garden, from which he sold vegetables to travelers and woodsmen. He had come to the area in 1849 from North Carolina. In 1850, he returned to North Carolina and interested his brother, John Ogburn and a friend, Isaac Shouse in returning to California with him. After a few years, Charlie returned to his home state. John Ogburn remained and married Emma Jones on November 10, 1856. John bought out his brother and continued to manage the ranch.

The Charlie's Place Ranch became a roadhouse, and a stopping place for emigrants. It was noted for its fine

KEN JOHNSTON

Charley's (Charlie's) Ranch
Photo by Author

Marker at Charlie's Place
Photo by Author

Nobles Emigrant Trail

peach brandy and quality blacksmithing. Later, bull and bear fights attracted crowds from all around, as far away as Sacramento and San Francisco. The Californios, as the Californians of Spanish descent were called, were the first to pit grizzly bears against bulls in California. The spectacles continued after California became a state and were finally outlawed in 1859.

Hubert Howe Bancroft, American historian and ethnologist, wrote in *California Pastoral*:

> A bull and bear fight after the sabbath services was indeed a happy occasion. It was a soul-refreshing sight to see the growling beasts of blood tied with a long raeta by one of its hind feet, as to leave it free to use its claws and teeth.

Jake Lee Hanne, in the October 23, 2017 online issue of *Atlas Obscura* continued the story.

> And there the spectators would find the vaqueros from the mountains clamping irons on the grizzly and blooding it with small dogs sacrificed to keep the bear in the mood.
>
> The bull and bear would be tied together by a long length of rope, but short enough to keep the two gladiators in each other's company. At the outset, the bear would usually hang back, taking a defensive posture on its hind legs, while the bull was often the first to attack, charging with head down and horns lethal.

KEN JOHNSTON

Bull and Bear Fight
Courtesy of Shasta Historical Society

Nobles Emigrant Trail

It was generally understood by eyewitness accounts that the bear held the advantage in the fray. While the bull had a deadly lunge, the bear could parry the advance and grab the bull by the head, sinking its teeth into the bull's neck, or on one account, biting the bull's tongue, which would have undoubtedly released a crowd-pleasing bellow.

At such times the vaqueros would jump in and break up the fight to save the bull and prolong the drama.

"I was present," stated a spectator named Arnaz in the pages of California Pastoral, *"when a bear killed three bulls." Often a single grizzly would fight many bulls consecutively until the home team won. "Sometimes the bull came off victorious, and at other times the bear, the result depending somewhat on the ages of the beasts."*

The fights were held in a log arena surrounded by a dry moat to protect spectators. Sometimes the bear was chained to the bull or to a post to prevent it from escaping, and often the bull's horns were sawed off to protect the more valuable bear.

When passing Charley's place on September 7, 1859, A.L. Covel wrote, "...past shingle town... past a sawmill... drove through a fine grove past the Gizley Bears Cage..."

Trinitarianus Chapter No. 62 of E. Clampus Vitus dedicated a unique wooden marker on Charlie's Place ranch property on April 23, 1983. The inscription reads:

KEN JOHNSTON

"In 1849 Charles Ogburn built a road to this site from Fort Reading. Ogburn's road later became part of the famed Noble Emigrant route. Ogburn built a cabin, planted orchards & later sold to his brother John in 1856. Charlie's Place was popular for its fine brandy & blacksmithing. Bear & bull fights promoted the family enterprise. In 1942, Herbert 'Ringtail' Johnson bought the ranch from the Ogburn heirs. The second house on this site, built in 1867, burned in 1952."

Across Highway 44 from Charlie's Ranch is the Ogburn Cemetery. The Ogburn family may have given some of their land, or perhaps land in the public domain next to theirs, which became the pioneer cemetery named in their honor. Harriet Ball's grave is located here (see page 183 for photo of her headstone).

From Charlie's Place, Nobles Trail closely followed Highway 44 west to Rancho Del Encino, owned by the great grand-nephew of John Sutter. It then turned down Dersch Road.

Nobles Emigrant Trail

Ogburn Cemetery
Photo by Author

KEN JOHNSTON

Foot-of-the-Mountain Station - The Schuler home
Courtesy of Shasta Historical Society

Nobles Emigrant Trail

Foot of the Mountain Station

Foot of the Mountain Station was a major stage and freight stop located about one mile north of the present Lack Creek Bridge on Dersch Road. It was about halfway between Charlie's Ranch and Dersch Ranch on the Nobles Trail. Also called Wayside Inn, it was a two and a half story pine building built by William L. (Billy) Smith in 1858. It was erected against a hillside that gave it its name. Reportedly a wild and rowdy place, the ground floor contained a barroom and gambling hall, and the second floor had a dance hall and six bedrooms. Smith held many gala affairs with some lasting as long as a week.[57]

After bankruptcy proceedings in 1865, it was deeded to Phoebe Colburn to pay off a debt. She was an emancipated black slave, who became a colorful character in Shasta

---
57 Smith, Dottie. *The Dictionary of Early Shasta County*. p. 79 & 80.

County history. Smith had employed Phoebe as a cleaning woman and housekeeper at the Foot of the Mountain Station. She had been frugal and saved her earnings. So, when Smith needed money, she loaned him $500. Later, Smith saw he could no longer make the station a paying business, and he turned it over to her for the $500 he owed her.

She then sold it to George Schuler in 1870. He remodeled it into his home and developed the surrounding land into the Schuler Ranch. According to Dottie Smith, "...the new owners quickly set about removing the blood stains in the floor and the bullet holes in the walls and ceilings."[58] Schuler covered the bullet holes with wallpaper, but reportedly could never completely get rid of the blood stains.

---

58   Smith, Dottie. "Travelin' in Time" April 15, 2010

Nobles Emigrant Trail

Bear Creek and Dersch Ranch

A journal entry by Joseph R. Bradway on September 12, 1853 is posted on the Trails West Marker here. It states,

> "Rolled, on to Bear Creek a distance of about 14 miles and encamped on a small island near the creek...many grapes nearly ripe along the banks and Grizzly Bears are said to be plenty."

Thus the name of the creek. A tent camping place was established on the banks in 1850 by "Doc" Baker. It became popular for emigrants, stages, and freight drovers, and in 1861 was purchased by George and Anna Marie Dersch.

Robert Amesbury gives us the following account.

> It was here that on August 22, 1866, a band of hostile Indians of the Yana tribe raided the Dersch place on Bear Creek, and killed Mrs. Anna Marie

KEN JOHNSTON

Trails West marker N-58 at Dersch Ranch
Photo by Author

Dersch Ranch house
Photo by Author

Nobles Emigrant Trail

Dersch, wife of George Dersch, who had settled the place in 1861. Present on the farm at the time of the tragedy were Mrs. Dersch, her daughter Anna and son Fred, and her brother in law Fred Dersch Sr. who was blind. When Mrs. Dersch was first shot through the right side, the ball going clear through, she screamed to the children to hide and she attempted to run but a second shot in the back felled her. One of the children was with the uncle in the orchard. Because of his sight impairment he could only stand helpless while his wounded sister in law screamed her life away.

The Shasta Courier of August 25, 1866, gave a report of this and said it was assumed she would die. By the time the report came out she had already passed away August 23. One of the routing posse told Mrs. McNamar the Indians went on the war path because Bill Pool the well known Indian fighter was living in the valley near the Dersches. Bill Pool claimed to have come on the scene while the Indians were still carousing and shot the Indian who shot Mrs. Dersch. Incidentally, this farm house was burned quite a number of years later, but was rebuilt almost exactly like the original house there at Bear Creek."[59]

---

[59] Amesbury p. 33 & 34.

KEN JOHNSTON

The Dersch Homestead marker inscription reads: "Here in 1850 'Doc' Baker established a stopping place for emigrants on what became known as the Nobles Trail. George and Anna Marie Dersch bought out Baker and homesteaded the land in 1861. Tenants of the Dersches were responsible for whipping three Indian laborers working on the potato harvest at the ranch. As a result of this incident, Indians raided the property in 1866, fatally wounding Mrs. Dersch. In retaliation, a posse was formed and killed most of the Indians at their Dye Creek camp. California Registered Landmark No.120."

Dersch Homestead Marker
Photo by Author

Robert L. Reid Jr. added information to the story: *About the middle of the 1850s an incident took place that could have*

NOBLES EMIGRANT TRAIL

started the Dersch massacre several years later. Doc Baker hired a large Missourian and his wife and two Indians to help harvest potatoes. The Indians were to receive their pay with potatoes. The wife said she saw the Indians go to their rancheria with bulges in their shirts. A whipping was decided upon. A neighbor rode up at the time. He was pushed into watching the whipping. The Indians said the wife had lied. One Indian had to watch the other whipped. The Missourian took over. He kicked his mouth until it was crushed, the Indian gave in after almost passing out from pain. Both Indians were freed, given potatoes, and told to come to work the next day. The grudge was carried for years and it caused the Indians to kill innocent as well as guilty.[60]

When Mrs. Dersch was killed, many of her neighbors and local citizens banded together and formed the infamous Millville Volunteers, a private militia that immediately set out to avenge her death.

---

60 Reid, Robert L. Jr. *"Study of Minorities in Shasta County, 1850-1880."* p. 51-52. 1969. CSU, Chico - Meriam Library. Abstract: Page 2-3: Boundaries of Indian culture; major general language groups, Wintun, Yana, Shastan, Modoc, and Northern Paiute.

Twin Bridges
Photo by Author

Nobles Emigrant Trail

Millville Plains Road and Twin Bridges

Twin Bridges were built in 1924 at the junction of Dersch Road and Millville Plains Road to cross the east and west channels of Dry Creek. They are important for their distinctive method of construction: "They are the only known examples in California of reinforced concrete slab bridges using reinforced concrete arches through railings."[61] But they are not important for their historical connection to the Nobles Trail.

Just north of Dersch Road and to the east of where Millville Plains Road intersects it, a historical marker designates the place where twin bridges cross the wash. To the north about five miles Millville was settled, as a farm, in 1853. In 1855, a flour mill was built by Drury D. Harrill. It supplied Shasta and neighboring counties with flour for years. A general store was added in 1857. For a while it was the second largest town in Shasta County.

---
61   Smith, Dottie. *The Dictionary of Early Shasta County.*

KEN JOHNSTON

William L. Allen and Catherine B. Allen lived at Basin Hollow near Millville on Cow Creek. Mrs. Allen was attacked at her home and killed by Indians in 1864. Mrs. John Jones was shot and killed the next day, presumably by the same Indians. In retaliation by settlers, hundreds of innocent Indians were massacred.[62]

Dottie Smith has noted that Catherine Allen, Mrs. John Jones, and Anna Marie Dersch who was killed two years later, all lived near Indian petroglyph sites. She suggests that their murders may have resulted from the beliefs of the local Indians that it was taboo for women to approach or be near their sacred sites, especially if it was the time of their monthly menstrual cycle.

Millville was also the site where "A Bull & Bear fight was held during the 1860s on a flat toward Clover Creek to which a large crowd of men attended (women were excluded). The bull was named Jeff Davis and the bear (brown) was named Abe Lincoln. The bull gored the bear to death. Betting was heavy and patriotism ran high. Supposedly the crowd lined up on whichever side their sympathies lay, and the fist fight that followed made the Bull & Bear fight look like a very mild affair."[63]

---

62 Ibid. p. 4.
63 Ibid p. 152.

Nobles Emigrant Trail

Cow Creek
and
Fort Reading

On the west side of Cow Creek, where Dersch Road crosses it, is a stone monument marking the site in the field to the north where Fort Reading, constructed out of adobe, had been located.

It was established on the west side of the creek in 1852 by the 2nd Infantry, with Lieutenant Nelson H. Davis in charge. It was named in honor of Pierson B. Reading, who held the first Mexican Land Grant in the area, and it was built to protect the mining district from Indian attack.

Unfortunately, malaria became a problem in the Sacramento Valley and, likewise, at the fort. The disease had been brought to America by European settlers and their West African slaves in the 16th century.

"In the fall of 1832, Hudson's Bay Company trappers unwittingly introduced malaria into the

mosquito-infested wetlands of central California. The Indian inhabitants had no immunity to the disease and died in huge numbers. By the late 1830s, the Bay Miwok nations had disappeared and the Valley Miwok nations in what is now northern San Joaquin County and southern Sacramento County had lost at least 80 per cent of their people to the epidemic."[64]

The Fort flooded often during the rainy season and was completely abandoned on April 6, 1870. "Fort Reading's soldiers were later moved to Fort Crook up in the lava country near Fall River Mills because of increased Indian trouble up there and the bad malaria condition at Ft. Reading."[65]

Fort Reading marker
Photo by Author

---

64   Stewart, David R. p. 11.
65   Amesbury p. 35.

Nobles Emigrant Trail

Sacramento Ferry

In 1852, Drury Harrill and Co. obtained a license to operate a ferry across the Sacramento River at the mouth of Cow Creek. This was known as the "Emigrant Ferry" and it served the travelers coming in from the east on the Nobles Trail. Remember this man, Harrill, was with the Nobles Party from Shasta on the initial trip to prove Nobles' claims. He was the one who lost his hat in the creek and Hat Creek was named at that time.

The Trails West marker N-59 is presently located under the south end of the Airport Road Bridge. It says:

"WE...MADE READY TO START FOR THE MINES. TWELVE MILES ON THE OTHER SIDE OF THE SACRAMENTO RIVER. WE CROSSED IN A BOAT, AND CAME TO CLEAR CREEK. TOSTEN KITTELSEN STABAEK, 1852."

After crossing the ferry, some of the emigrants headed south to Red Bluff while others continued west and then northwest about seven miles to the "diggings" along Clear Creek. Many of the emigrants were not interested in mining and they continued northwest to Shasta City where lodging and supplies were readily available.

Location of the Emigrant Ferry over Sacramento River on the Nobles Trail, with Trails West marker N-59.
Photo by Author

Nobles Emigrant Trail

Clear Creek

About half way from the ferry to Canon House, Highway 273 crosses Clear Creek. Upstream from that location is where Pierson B. Reading discovered gold at Reading's Bar in the spring of 1849, leading to the Shasta Gold Rush. Thousands of people rushed to the area.

Boomtowns of tents, cabins, or shacks soon sprang up with miners living a sparse existence while working their claims. Horsetown, Muletown, Jackass Flat, Middletown, Centerville, Texas Springs, Shasta Gulch, Buljin Gulch, Igo, Piety Hill, and Briggsville were some of the creative names the miners came up with for their towns. Few remain today. Fires, dredging, and submersion by water destroyed them. Whiskeytown was submerged by Whiskeytown Reservoir.

Supplies for the towns were shipped by boat to Red Bluff and hauled by freight wagons to Horsetown and Shasta. The towns may be gone, but their history remains to be discovered in the museums and libraries of the area.

Trails West marker N-60
Photo by Author

Nobles Emigrant Trail

Canon House and Graves

The Trails West Marker N-60 stands beside the Fire Station on the southwest corner of Highway 273 and Buenaventura Street. It is all that remains to denote the significance of the historic Canon House. The House, a two-story wooden building with a wooden veranda across the front, was a wayside inn in the early 1850s, and was the last stopping place on the Nobles Trail before travelers reached their destination at Shasta City.

On December 19, 1853, two men, named Jones and Catey, bought the building and 160 acres from Major Pierson B. Reading. It was part of the original Buena Ventura land grant that Reading received from Governor Micheltorena in 1844 (while California was still Mexican territory) and patented in 1857.

George Jones and Mr. Catey married sisters, who were both daughters of Frederick and Rebecca McIntosh who had come to California from Kentucky with ten children. Jones married Sydnia Ann. Catey, a partner in the Canon House business, married Elizabeth Ann, Sydnia's sister.

The McIntoshes were visiting Canon House in May of 1864 in anticipation of the birth of Jones and Sydnia's first daughter. On May 16, Frederick McIntosh was hunting and shot a hare. While he was trying to retrieve the animal from under a bush by using his shotgun, it discharged, sending the load of shot through his wrist and exiting from his elbow. Physicians had to amputate his lower arm. While he was recovering from the wound, he allegedly died of typhoid fever.

Frederick was a Mason and an Oddfellow. He was a friend of Peter Lassen and Major Reading, who were also Masons. He was given a proper burial, and his grave is located nearby where the Canon house stood. His daughter, Elizabeth Ann Catey died three months later, and her grave is beside his.[66]

Unfortunately, the house and graves no longer exist— only the spirits of the place remain. They are nearly obscured today by the hustle and bustle of nearby traffic.

---

66   Hollenbeck, Edna. p. 40

NOBLES EMIGRANT TRAIL

SHASTA CITY OR OLD SHASTA

Originally named Upper Reading Springs in honor of Pierson B. Reading, it was founded in 1849. The town was renamed Shasta on June 8, 1850, and it became known as the "Queen City of the North." It was, for a time between 1851-1888, the county seat for Shasta County. It was the largest settlement in Shasta County and California north of Sacramento. Here, until 1861, the road ended and the Oregon pack trail began.

Shasta, being near the rich mines and back country, was actually more a stage stop and shipping center than a mining town until 1872, when the railroad extended to the town of Redding. Up to one hundred mule trains and teams were reported to have arrived at Shasta some days.

Shasta's first settlers were mostly miners involved in placer mining. According to the *Shasta Courier* of 24 November 1855, the population was about 5,000 and the completion of a forty-mile long Clear Creek Ditch brought another 2,000 miners to the area.

One of California's best-preserved ghost towns—with

Remanants of Shasta City ghost town
Photo by Author

Trails West marker N-61
Photo by Author

many interpretive signs—is a truly romantic ruin where brick walls support iron shutters that still swing on old iron hinges. The roofless buildings have been stabilized. The building that was once the Shasta County Courthouse has been restored and now houses a museum with historical exhibits for the Shasta State Historic Park. In the back of the building is a jail and scaffolding where hangings had taken place. The original jail was a log affair. It is reported to have had the famous poet of the Sierras, Joaquin Miller, among its many prisoners in 1859, allegedly for stealing horses.

The Western Star Lodge #2 is the oldest Masonic Lodge in California. Its charter was brought to California from Missouri in 1848 by Saschel Woods as Master, Lucien E. Stewart as Senior Warden, and Peter Lassen as Junior Warden. Saschel Woods had custody of the Charter. He came to California in Lassen's wagon train of 1848. He held the first Masonic meeting on October 30, 1849 at Benton City on Lassen's Rancho.

The lodge was later moved to Shasta City in 1851 and became Western Star Lodge #2. (The lodge in San Francisco was erroneously given the designation as Lodge #1.) The Masonic Hall in Shasta City was built in 1853 and continues to be used for meetings today.

There were about five thousand Chinese in the Shasta area. It was one of the largest Chinese populations in the state in 1853. They played a large role in the Gold Rush, as they were very efficient miners and were able to extract gold where other miners had worked and moved on.

The Chinese customs, food, and religion were very different, and they typically kept to themselves in Chinatowns that existed on the outskirts of many mining camps. Their section in Shasta was known as Hong Kong. It had a hotel, gambling dens, saloons, stores, a Joss House (a Chinese temple or shrine),[67] and a Chinese cemetery.

---

67 An original Joss House still exists and can be visited in Weaverville west on Hwy 299. It is part of a State Park.

KEN JOHNSTON

The white miners' resentment and racism of the Chinese grew, and resulted in the expulsion of the Chinese from Horsetown, Muletown, and Shasta. "Mysteriously," most of the Chinatown in Shasta was destroyed by fire so that little evidence of their legacy is left.

In 1851, the Shasta county seat was moved from Major Reading's Ranch and remained in Shasta City until 1888, when it was moved to the town of Redding also known as "Poverty Flat."[68]

Shasta also suffered three devastating fires. The last one in 1878, along with the decreasing production of gold, resulted in the ultimate decline of the town.

Shasta City Marker   *Photo by Author*

End of the Nobles Trail in Shasta City.

---

68 Benjamin Bernard Redding, a politician and the person the town of Redding was named after, purchased property in Poverty Flat. Many people claim the city of Redding should have been named Reading after Pierson B. Reading who had originally obtained the land in a Mexican land grant.

1851-1852

Nobles Emigrant Trail

William Nobles promoted the Nobles Trail to the merchants of Shasta City in 1852 as being "a good wagon road from this place to the Humboldt river...which will be shorter and in every respect more practicable than any other overland immigrant route into California."

Nobles claimed credit for the discovery, and the merchants of Shasta City paid him $2,000 for revealing the route to them. But, Peter Lassen claimed he knew the route long before Nobles came to the area. Speculation and controversy still persist to this day about which of them actually "discovered" the route.

According to Robert Amesbury, William H. Nobles "...came into Honey Lake Valley or was guided by Peter Lassen with a band of 80 men in the spring of 1851. He probably heard and believed the story which Bruff recorded."

That story in Bruff's account revealed:

> There were amongst us an individual who knew a man, who not long since traveling to California, started with 5 companions from somewhere about Mud Lakes (Black Rock Desert) leaving the emigrant road there to reach California by a cutoff—a diagonal beeline—and he found a lake deeply basined in the mountains with plenty of golden pebbles and hostile Indians near the headwaters of the Yuba." [69]

Was Nobles interested in the gold when he went to Honey Lake Valley, or was he more interested in the "cutoff"? At any rate, Tim Purdy, Susanville historian, wrote, "At that point, Nobles and Lassen parted company."[70]

There is little written record of Lassen's activities in 1851 other than he was living in Indian Valley and had a trading post that provided vegetables and supplies for the prospectors who were pouring into the valley in search of gold. Was he away from his business exploring, and actually guiding Nobles and his party? Or was he just available to give advice to Nobles and other prospectors and explorers who passed through?

Whichever, Nobles must have explored the route through Smoke Creek Desert to the emigrant road (Applegate/Lassen trail) at Mud Lakes. Thus, he would have scouted and confirmed the true "cutoff' that so many 49ers and Bruff had expected.

However, according to *Hutching's California Magazine*, Nobles' proposed route at this time would

---

69   Amesbury..p. 4. and Bruff's journal entry Sept. 13, 1850.
70   Purdy, Tim. *At a Glance A Susanville History*. p. 7 & 8.

Nobles Emigrant Trail

have met the Lassen Trail at Lassen's Big Meadows. These meadows were just to the west of what was to become known as Nobles Pass.[71] However, when Nobles intersected the Lassen Trail at Lassen's Big Meadows, he continued on the Lassen Trail to Lassen's Rancho following the Lassen Route. Apparently, Nobles did not yet know of the pass or route north of Mount Lassen that his road would later follow—the road that Lassen would claim he knew first.

Not finding Lassen at his rancho, but learning he was in San Francisco, Nobles then went on to Gerke's in San Francisco, where Lassen was at the time. This causes one to wonder why he would have made this great detour, if indeed, his intention was to show Lassen a route he knew to Shasta City. His apparent intent was to discuss the establishment of ranches along the route. Did he already have in mind profiting from the route to Shasta?

> Swartzlow in *Lassen, His Life and Legacy,* wrote,
> *Lassen's interest in emigrant roads into California continued. In* Hutching's California Magazine *for 1856-57 an article entitled "A Jaunt to Honey Lake Valley and Noble's Pass" gives a description of the country and newer trail from the Humboldt River to the Sacramento Valley by way of Honey Lake Valley, known generally as Nobles' Road. The author states that Peter Lassen discovered Honey Lake in 1850*

---

71 According to *Fairfield's Pioneer History Of Lassen County, California.* P. 18, referencing *Hutching's California Magazine* June, 1857 article "Lassen's Big Meadows, was the west end of Noble's pass; and that the old settlers of Indian Valley claimed that to Peter Lassen is due the honor of having discovered the Noble's pass route, having known it long before Noble saw it."

and that he was the guide for William H. Nobles in 1851 on the first exploration of Nobles route. He traversed, then, a good portion of the National Park which now bears his name.[72]

Lassen had previously been over the area north of Mount Lassen (then known as Snow Butte) twice in 1846 when going after John C. Frémont, and then returning with him to Lassen's Rancho. According to Bruff, on August 12, 1850, "Lassen's expedition, rode in [to Lassen's base camp near the headwaters of the Feather River]...They had traveled to Cow Creek, found a lake at its head, & several others; been around the Snow Butte..."[73]

Perhaps this was when Lassen, according to "legendary truths," was the "first person" to climb the peak that was to later bear his name, although there is no documentation to support this, other than, "Grove K. Godfrey, who ascended the peak in the summer of 1851, states in an article he wrote in *Hutching's California Magazine* in 1860 that Peter Lassen was the first white man to climb the peak."[74]

Swartzlow went on to speculate that Lassen may have claimed that honor when, as she wrote, "It is reported by Godfrey that he and his group met Peter Lassen between Indian Valley and the North Fork of the Feather River. He [Lassen] had with him a small pack train carrying provisions and merchandise to his store in Indian Valley."[75]

---

72 *Lassen, His Life and Legacy.* p. 72. Note: In the Court Transcripts of Charles L. Wilson & John Wilson vs. Peter Lassen & Henry Gerke, October 5, 1853. Pomeroy testified that Lassen and Nobles left on an expedition in February of 1852, and "The business of the party was to explore a new route through the mountains."
73 Read & Gaines. p 382.
74 Johnston. p. 76.
75 Ibid. p. 76.

Nobles Emigrant Trail

In *Fairfield's Pioneer History of Lassen County, California*, he questioned that Nobles Trail went through Lassen's Big Meadows, which he was correct in questioning. Nobles' discovered route ended just east of the meadows, but later would follow the Lassen Trail north, to where it branched west and continued over the mountains north of Mount Lassen. In referring to *Hutching's California Magazine* article, Fairfield wrote:

> A part of the foregoing, at least, is certainly a mistake. The Noble route never went through Big Meadows and down Deer creek; and if Lassen knew that route, he must have found it after he made the Lassen Trail. It doesn't seem reasonable to suppose that if he knew of the Noble's pass route, he would take a party of emigrants up to Oregon and back, just to get from the Black Rock peak to Mt. Meadows. If he did, he should have been punished for it.[76]

However, according to later court testimonies, it is evident that Nobles actually did go through Big Meadows and down Deer Creek to Lassen's Rancho, and then to San Francisco to meet with Lassen, before Nobles developed his route around the north side of Mount Lassen.

Interestingly, Tom Hunt's essay in *A Guide To Nobles Trail*, edited by Richard K. Brock and Robert S. Black, also quoted the June 1857 *Hutching's California Magazine*:

> Most persons are well aware...[of] the emigration on what is known as Noble's Route—(Peter Lassen however

---

[76] Fairfield. p. 18. Note, this was four years after Lassen pioneered his trail, and it was due to later explorations that the newer route was discovered. Someone can't be punished in "retrospect."

> *it is claimed by the old settlers in Indian Valley, is entitled to that honor, having known it long before Mr. Noble ever saw it, and moreover was his guide all through this route, Mr. N. being entirely unacquainted with it.) This Mr. Lassen himself solemnly affirmed in our hearing, and so to us; and we make mention of it now that honor may be given where honor is most due.*[77]

But Tom Hunt went on to question,

> *Was Lassen here taking credit with the writer of this article for something he hadn't done, that is, taking credit for opening yet a second historic trail into California? Or was this just an example of "Old Pete" embroidering the historical record by playing loosely with the facts, simply because he knew that there was nobody around some five years after the opening of the Nobles Trail who could challenge his claim? Or then again was it possible that Lassen had, indeed, piloted Nobles along the basic Nobles Trail route in conjunction with one of his own journeys of exploration through the country in question?*[78]

Hunt referred to the transcript of trial testimonies from the court ruling on a lawsuit filed against Peter Lassen and Henry Gerke by John Wilson and Charles Wilson, dated October 5, 1853. From the testimonies, Hunt concluded,

77 Tom Hunt's essay in Brock & Black, p. 5
78 Ibid. p. 5.

Nobles Emigrant Trail

"The doubt raised by the above-cited 1857 *Hutching's California Magazine* article can finally be laid to rest. 'Old Pete' was, indeed, coveting more than the honor that was due him."[79]

Thus published, it adds to the "legendary truths" about Peter Lassen. But, in this case, as in others, are they more "true" than the truth itself?[80]

Nobles claimed to have hired a couple of men at $8 each per day for eight months to assist him in finding a better route over the mountains. In a letter that Nobles wrote to Jacob Thompson, Secretary of the Interior, dated April 16, 1852, he stated, "In February... I commenced at a point from 80 to 100 miles of Walkers Pass in the Southern end of the Sierra Nevada's and passing through the summits thoroughly explored the whole range to the Columbia River, which resulted in the discovery of a pass [Nobles Pass] in that range of mountains...."[81]

Considering that snow depths linger on the Sierra passes long into the summer, the distances Nobles would have had to travel to meet his claims of "passing through the summits thoroughly explored the whole range to the Columbia River," and also the time it would have taken to cover these great distances—even over some passes that hadn't yet been opened—his claims for travel and expenses seem so preposterous, that one historian wrote "...the complete letter is quite self-serving," and "...being

---

79 Ibid. p.7
80 At the time of publication of this book, Tom Hunt and some historians still question whether Lassen guided Nobles or whether Nobles showed Lassen the route.
81 Letter found by Tom Hunt in the National Archives and Records Administration, Interior Department Records. p. 1. "February" must refer to the year 1851, and in the winter of 1851 Nobles proposed showing the pass that had already been found to Lassen, Gerke, and others in San Francisco.

a promoter at heart, Nobles was prone to exaggeration on his behalf."[82]

The cost to Nobles for two men at $8/day for eight months [from February, from when Nobles claimed to have started, until November, when he reported his find in San Francisco] would total $3,840 just for their wages, not including other expenses. He must have been referring to 1851, as it was in that year that he went to Gerke's and reported finding his pass in November.

Later, Nobles asked the merchants of Shasta City for $2,000 as a payment for showing them his newly discovered route. Tom Hunt wrote that Nobles, "was one of the smart ones who saw the advantages of mining the miners, and his payment of $2,000 was undoubtedly more than most gold miners accumulated from their mining activities."[83]

According to an editor's comment in *A Guide To The Nobles Trail*, Nobles' payment of "$2,000 in 1852 was the equivalent of $49,280 in 2007."[84] So this was indeed a large amount of money, as Hunt pointed out. But using the same equation of $1 in 1852 = $24.64 in 2007, and using Nobles' claim of paying $8/day each to two men for eight months, his cost, as stated above, would have come to $3,840, or in 2007 dollars, $94,617.60—just for wages, not including costs for equipment, food, animals for transportation, and other desiderata and incidentals.

This accounting of Nobles exploring with two men doesn't fit with the previously mentioned statement by Amesbury that Nobles "...came into Honey Lake Valley or

---

82   Buck, Don. "William Nobles Itinerary In Opening The Nobles Trail From St. Paul, Minnesota Territory, to Shasta City, California, 1850-1852" Non-published paper, p 2.
83   Brock, Black. p. 4.
84   Ibid. p 7.

was guided by Peter Lassen with a band of 80 men in the spring of 1851," who were looking for Gold Lake.

It isn't surprising, therefore, that when Nobles returned back East to promote his road, it wasn't long before he was embroiled in accusations of misappropriating federal funds and property, land speculation, extravagance, and procrastination. Historian Jackson concluded that Nobles proved himself utterly incapable of mastering the necessary technical details associated with the administration of a federal government project.

It may still be controversial as to who discovered the route. But considering the following evidence as to Nobles' character and predilection to exaggeration and self-aggrandizement, as opposed to the testimonies toward Lassen's integrity and honesty, one would conclude that Lassen was the one who should receive the credit. The evidence includes:

1) The June, 1857, edition of *Hutching's California Magazine* article stating that Lassen was the discoverer of the route as claimed by the "old settlers of Indian Valley," and "solemnly affirmed" by Mr. Lassen; [85]

2) A *Red Bluff Beacon* article on October 27, 1858, which said that "whoever shakes the hand of Peter Lassen shakes the hand of an honest man"; [86] and

3) Swartzlow's tribute, "There is no indication that he [Lassen] was morally less than circumspect," and "...Peter Lassen was an honest and forthright man."[87]

It therefore seems likely that the reports were true that Nobles was either guided by Lassen over part of the way

---

85   Tom Hunt's essay in Brock & Black,. p. 5
86   *Lassen: His Life and Legacy.* p. 44.
87   Ibid. p 79 & 9.

or he at least consulted with Lassen before he met with the proposed "company" at Gerke's in the fall of 1851. In the words of Ruby Swartzlow, "He [Lassen] was consulted by soldiers, travelers, and emigrants because they relied on his familiarity with the terrain."[88] So, at the time that Nobles was looking for a new route, he surely would have sought out Lassen.

Tom Hunt wrote, "Furthermore, both men had to have been active in the same geographical area in the early 1850's. It is hard to imagine Nobles, who was determined to open a new and better route into California, not searching out Lassen and availing himself of that trail pioneer's store of knowledge."[89]

Indeed, if we scrutinize the transcript of the Wilson/Lassen trial testimonies more carefully, we read that in the fall of 1851 (probably after having explored the Nobles Route from the Mud Lakes [Black Rock] to Lassen's Big Meadows), Nobles, along with Peter Lassen, Henry Gerke, C.C. Catlett, General A. Hudson, I. L. Van Bokelyn, St. Felix, Messersmith, and others, met at Gerke's home in San Francisco. Their purpose was to form a company to promote the new, shorter route, develop ranches along it, and monopolize trade with incoming emigrants.

In the court transcripts, as Tom Hunt indicated, Nobles wanted to establish ranches along the route and "to turn a tidy profit." Since Lassen's Rancho was at the terminus, it would "effectively give the proposed company a complete monopoly of trade along the route."[90]

Lassen produced papers to this company about his ranch, supposedly to get the company's help in clearing his entanglement with the Wilsons. Messersmith later testified:

88   Ibid. p. 74.
89   Tom Hunt's essay in Brock & Black. p. 5.
90   Ibid. p.6.

Nobles Emigrant Trail

Was at Gerke's home at the time St Felix, Van Bokelyn, Lassen & others were there in the winter of [1851 and] 1852. I remember Lassen wished to join our Company & produce papers there about his Ranch which were read over;...The Lassen Ranch had nothing to do with the matter of our Company at its origin. The object of the Company was to explore Nobles pass and locate Ranches on the line of it...I never heard of the Lassen Ranch until after the Return of some of our party from up Country. Then heard Lassen had made propositions to Nobles to come in & join our Company. Have no interest in the Lassen Ranch.[91]

Note, the "Nobles pass" referred to here was the area west of Susanville along the Susan River, east of where the Nobles route joined the Lassen Trail east of Mount Lassen. Nobles was seeking help in "locating Ranches on the line of it."

Apparently, at this time, Lassen was interested in trying to enlist their help in ousting the Wilsons from his rancho. Tom Hunt wrote that Nobles and the others could not satisfy Lassen's request to get rid of the Wilsons, so the deal collapsed.[92]

Because of this or some other reason, Nobles decided to further his explorations and take his road around the north side of Mount Lassen and end it at Shasta City, rather than at Lassen's Rancho. To do this, he later met with Lassen at Rancho Bosquejo to explore the route.

91 Court Transcripts of Charles L. Wilson & John Wilson vs. Peter Lassen & Henry Gerke. October 5, 1853. Historic Records in Sacramento, Calif. Witness Testimonies. p. 70 & 71.
92 Tom Hunt's essay in Brock & Black. p. 6 & 7.

KEN JOHNSTON

Mr. Pomeroy testified:

> *I think he [Lassen] left again in February and was gone only a few days. He was to explore a new pass [not to be confused with Nobles Pass, which was east of Mount Lassen and ended at Lassen's Big Meadows[93]]. The party consisted of Lassen, Noble, Gerke, Hudson, Van Bokelyn, Smith and St. Felix. This was February 1852. The business of the party was to explore a new route through the mountains. I never heard any dissatisfaction [presumably dissatisfaction with the Wilsons] on the part of Lassen until after this party arrived at the ranch it was about the time that Gerke & Noble arrived. I think Gerke came up on the second trip of the Comanche.*[94]

When Pomeroy was cross-examined, he referred to his job as bookkeeper at Lassen's Rancho and expenses for the exploration on the pass over the mountains:

> *...Mr. Lassen was charged at his own request with the board of the exploring party with the exception of Gerke. He said he did not want Gerke charged anything as he was a particular friend of his and that he always stopped at*

---

93 Note: "Lassen's Big Meadows was the west end of Noble's pass," according to *Fairfield's Pioneer History Of Lassen County, California,* referencing the *Hutching's California Magazine* article.

94 Court Transcripts of Charles L. Wilson & John Wilson vs. Peter Lassen & Henry Gerke. October 5, 1853. Historic Records in Sacramento, Calif. Witness Testimonies. p. 66 & 67.

NOBLES EMIGRANT TRAIL

his (Gerkes') house when down at San Francisco with out any charge being made for it."[95]

If "the new pass" Nobles already knew of was the route around the north side of Mount Lassen, why hadn't he gone directly to Fort Reading and Shasta City rather than going all the way to San Francisco to meet with Lassen and men associated with him and his rancho? (Note: Lassen's rancho was at the end of the established road Nobles probably followed from Nobles Pass and Lassen's Big Meadows directly into the Sacramento Valley.)

Why did Nobles go out of his way and waste more time with Lassen and the others who could not "satisfy Lassen's request to get rid of Wilson" or "locate Ranches on the line of it [Nobles Trail]"?

Later, in the spring of 1852, after the "exploring party" found the "pass" through the mountains, and Lassen had shown him the route north of the mountain, William Nobles convinced the merchants of Shasta City, California (near present day Redding), that he had discovered a viable wagon road to their thriving town.

As stated before, for the consideration of $2,000 Nobles agreed to show the businessmen of Shasta City the new wagon route that initially branched off the Applegate Trail at Black Rock, and headed southwest across the Black Rock and Smoke Creek Deserts to Honey Lake Valley and Susanville. From there the trail continued westerly through forested and volcanic country, crossing the mountains on the north flank of Mount Lassen, and, finally descended into the upper end of the Sacramento Valley, near Fort Reading, and terminated at Shasta City.

The Nobles Trail became one of the easiest of all the

---

95 Ibid. p. 68.

wagon routes into northern California, and it received heavy use in subsequent years.[96]

To date, the only resolution to the controversy as to which of these two men discovered the route, depends on what can be deduced from the following:

1. Nobles Trail intersected the Lassen Trail at Lassen's Big Meadow in 1851;
2. William Nobles went to Gerke's in Yerba Buena (San Francisco) to discuss with Lassen the possibility of locating ranches along the route;
3. Lassen's "solemn affirmation" that he was Nobles' guide all through this route;
4. Many testimonials as to Lassen's honesty;
5. Claims of "old settlers" that Peter Lassen was "due the honor of having discovered the Noble's pass route, having known it long before Noble saw it";
6. Newspaper articles; and
7. Interpretation of testimonies in the Wilson/Lassen Court Trial as opposed to Nobles' claim, based on a self-aggrandizing letter that he wrote two months later. After returning to Lassen's rancho and going over the mountains with Lassen, Nobles went to Shasta City.

---

96 The Nobles Trail was designated as part of the California National Historic Trail by Act of Congress in the 1992 Pony Express and California National Historic Trails Act. For more information on the trail, go to www.blm.gov/ca/st/en/fo/eaglelake/nobles.html

Nobles Emigrant Trail

Other Contributing Discoveries to the Route

The Nobles Trail began at Black Rock, and crossed Mud Lake, also called the Black Rock Desert, to Granite Station north of where Gerlach, Nevada is today. However, a second, shorter route was later discovered that began just beyond Rabbit Hole Springs going more directly to Granite Station by Trego Hot Springs and Coyote Spring, and not going all the way to Black Rock.

The Nobles Trail considerably shortened the Lassen Trail and intersected it just east of Mount Lassen, avoiding the long detour of the "Horn Route" as the Lassen Trail had been called by some disgruntled emigrants, referring to its long detour to the north.

Striking the Lassen Trail just west of Nobles Pass, it then followed the Lassen Trail north past Feather Lake and turned up Butte Creek, entering the northeast corner of the Lassen Volcanic National Park. It then passed north of the

KEN JOHNSTON

Cinder Cone, and crossed an area that would later become known as the Devastated Area due to the eruption of Mount Lassen that would happen on May 21, 1915. It then entered Sunflower Flat just north of Mount Lassen and the Chaos Crags, crossed the Chaos Jumbles, passed Manzanita Lake, and continued to Deer Flat.

The section between Chaos Crags and Table Mountain became known as Emigrant Pass or Nobles Second Pass. It was the route presumably shown to Nobles by Lassen in February of 1852. Lassen had crossed this area in 1846 when going in search of Frémont, and again in 1850 (as documented by Bruff) when prospecting for Gold Lake.

Lassen claimed to have shown Nobles this section. Probably rightly so, but in no way did Lassen "discover" this route. He only claimed to have shown Nobles the route. The Hudson Bay Trappers had traveled the route from Cow (Canoe) Creek to Hat Creek on trapping expeditions for years. And Lassen had followed the route in 1846 when guiding Lt. Gillespie to Klamath Lake to meet with John C. Frémont.

Also, Lassen had explored around the north side of Lassen Peak in 1850 while looking for the mythological Gold Lake, and he had gone as far as Cow Creek.[97]

Somewhere near Deer Flat, roads to the McCumber Mill area had already been established from Fort Reading and Shasta City. With the influx of prospectors into the Redding and Shasta City areas, there was a great demand for cedar shingles and sugar pine shakes. Since there was an ample supply of trees east of Redding, roads had already been established to Shingle Camp (later to become Shingletown) and on to Deer Flat before Lassen and Nobles arrived in February 1852. These roads then became the last section of the Nobles Trail.

---

97 Bruff, Aug. 12, 1850

Nobles Emigrant Trail

The twenty-four mile section of trail within the boundaries of Lassen Volcanic National Park was placed on the National Register of Historic Places on October 3, 1975. The section within the Park is maintained as a hiking trail. The trail within the Park starts in the northeast corner and passes between Prospect Peak and the Cinder Cone. It crosses Badger Flat and the area devastated by the 1915 eruption of Lassen Peak. It then passes to the north of Chaos Crags going through Chaos Jumbles and into the Old Summertown area, and it leaves the Park near Manzanita Lake.

However, in 1855 an alternate route from Butte Creek Meadows over the Hat Creek Rim and up the Hat Creek Valley to the Manzanita Lake area avoided the heavy volcanic ash on the trail near the Cinder Cone and the seasonal heavy snows. This alternative resulted from the development of the Lockhart Road connecting Red Bluff to Yreka in 1855. It took wagons from the Deer Flat Area over Eskimo Hill, down the Hat Creek valley, and crossed the Pit River to the north on the Lockhart Ferry.

KEN JOHNSTON

Nobles Emigrant Trail

Early Hints of a Trail Through Smoke Creek

As in other places throughout the West, Smoke Creek Desert and Smoke Creek Canyon provided a natural route through the mountains that animal trails and Native Americans had followed from time immemorial and were well established before explorers and emigrant leaders arrived in the West.

In early January of 1844, the John C. Frémont Party rode south through High Rock Canyon into the Black Rock Desert. They discovered and camped by the Great Boiling Springs near where the town of Gerlach, Washoe County, Nevada, would later be built. It was on the edge of the large, barren playa of the Black Rock Desert they called Mud Lake, and it would later be referred to as Mud Lake in the journals of emigrants traversing the area in 1849.

KEN JOHNSTON

On January 7 of 1844 Frémont left the Hot Springs with Kit Carson and Alexis Godey to explore for a route through the mountains to California. They rode south and west into the Smoke Creek Desert, finding and following what appeared to be a well-used trail. Frémont wrote that they found a ravine where there was water and grass. They camped there and saw tracks of unshod horses.

They continued southwest, apparently separating and taking different directions for a time. Later reports told of them finding pure water, a good covering of grass, and groves of cottonwoods. It isn't known how far west Carson traveled or if he could possibly have gone up Smoke Creek Canyon. And there is no mention of Godey's travels in the area, but Godey's Rock and Godey's Gap west of the Great Boiling Springs still retain his name.

On January 10, speculation has it that near the end of the Smoke Creek Basin, Carson had traveled up a mountain hollow to Emerson Pass. Some historians claim it was there that he first saw a large mountain lake before hurrying back to reconnoiter with Frémont and his party as they were heading south into the San Emidio Desert south of the Black Rock.

Carson told Frémont of the lake and the party changed their direction, crossing from San Emidio Canyon by Kits Peak into Sweetwater Canyon to reach the amazing body of water they would later name Pyramid Lake. They named it after they'd camped by a large pyramid shaped rock in the lake that reminded Frémont of the great pyramid at Cheops in Egypt. Frémont even thought that the lake might possibly be the source of the fabled Buenaventura River.

Note: at this time, there was some exploration west of the Great Boiling Springs on the route that would later become known as the Nobles Trail. Also, similar claims of

Nobles Emigrant Trail

early knowledge of the area will repeatedly come up in the future and lead to further speculation and mystique.

Interestingly, back in 1844, an "old mountain man" Bill Williams, after trapping in the Klamath Lake and Tule Lake country and having problems with the Modoc Indians, led his party of forty trappers, including William Thomas Hamilton, southward to Honey Lake. They spent most of the spring of 1844 hunting and trapping in northern Nevada, and reportedly passed Pyramid Lake. He was also a friend of Alexis Godey and Kit Carson, who had been in the area also in 1844 with Frémont. Did they also travel to or through the Smoke Creek area?[98]

It is interesting to speculate about other mountain men, trappers, and early explorers who may have passed through this area, and either never recorded their presence or their recordings haven't yet been found.

In 1845 and 1846, Richard (Dick) Owens, a close friend of both Kit Carson and Alexis Godey, later traveled with them and Frémont to California. Returning east in 1847, General Kearny, was escorting Frémont to a court martial, for insubordination that he has accused Frémont of. After crossing Truckee Pass, they passed the camp and gruesome remains of the Donner Party. (The previous year, the Donner Party of eighty seven members was trapped on the pass by deep snow, and only forty eight survived—some by resorting to cannibalism.)

It is likely members of the Stephen Watts Kearny party, including Frémont, Kit Carson, and Dick Owens, were so affected by what they saw at the Donner site, they then told all westbound wagons they met that they should avoid the Truckee Route and its potential dangers and follow the Applegate Trail north.

---

98   Favour, Alpheus and Hamilton, William Thomas.

KEN JOHNSTON

Two weeks after Kearny and Frémont went east over the Donner Summit, Commodore Stockton, accompanied by Peter Lassen, Milton McGee, John J. Myers, and many others who would be trail guides during the Gold Rush of 1849, also passed the Donner camps. They made similar recommendations to those they met. Peter Lassen in 1848, and McGee and Myers in 1849, later followed this advice when leading their own emigrant parties West.

Owens would probably have gained some knowledge of the earlier explorations of Frémont's Party, and possibly had some idea of the lay of the land that the newly discovered Applegate Trail traversed in going to the Black Rock Desert and Smoke Creek area where the Frémont Party had been in January of 1844.

Was the new route discussed when they approached the area south of Pyramid Lake and also where the Applegate Trail turned north from the Humboldt? Could Dick Owens have discussed the area with Carson and Frémont?

Later, in 1849, Dick Owens would lead a Cherokee Party pack train through the area. Did he apply the knowledge to head directly west from the Black Rock following the significant Indian trails? If Dick Owens did indeed lead his pack train through Smoke Creek, as some historians speculate, this would explain the journal entries recorded by the emigrants on the Lassen Trail who expected to find the "Cherokee Cutoff."

NOBLES EMIGRANT TRAIL

THE CHEROKEE CUTOFF

Another confusing but provocative story exists about a "Cherokee Cutoff" that was recorded by Israel Lord in his journal on September 9, 1849.

> *Lay over...We are laying in for a long drive without grass... Report here says that there are four routes, the old one, across the desert; another, striking Truckey River twelve miles north lower down; a third north of Pyramid Lake, by Mud Lake, crossing over to Feather River; and a fourth, still further north, called Government Road. The last two leave the road about sixty miles below, at the next great bend of the river.*
>
> *The first of these two is called the Cherokee route, and promises so much that, if I mistake not, it will be*

> *a humbug. A Cherokee who resides in California has been through to this point, and started back with the great Cherokee train, as it is now called, of one hundred wagons. The real Cherokee train was reduced to a dozen wagons, I should think, before this maneuver. This man reports a good route across the desert, and water and grass at some points.*
>
> *If there was not a northern route besides this into California, I certainly should not venture. If it should fail, the Government route is sure, though certainly far round. I shall consider it. All the men, I find, are determined to go that way; and probably any attempt to take the old route would lead to a division of the train. There are one hundred and fifty wagons in sight, preparing for hard times, and others rolling in hourly...*[99]

This is "provocative," but it also raises some questions. The "Government route"[100] he refers to is apparently the Lassen/Applegate route farther north. Israel Lord already knew that it "is sure, though certainly far round," indicating an awareness of the Lassen Route and its distance.

But, the Cherokee Cutoff goes "north of Pyramid Lake, by Mud Lake, crossing over to Feather River." This

---

99 Israel Lord Journal, 1849.
100 The term "Government Road" may have derived from the fact that Lieutenant Hawkins had led a government supply train from Oregon to Fort Hall over the Applegate/Lassen Route and met westbound emigrants with news about the road.

Nobles Emigrant Trail

describes the Lassen Trail, which passes Mud Lake north of Black Rock Desert just before entering High Rock Canyon.

If the Cherokee Cutoff followed a more direct path north of Pyramid Lake, it would probably have gone more directly west on the route later to be called the Nobles Trail. Again, there is some confusion here, because in many of the journals and on modern maps, the area near High Rock Canyon is referred to as Mud Lake, which the Lassen Trail clearly goes through. But, Frémont and others referred to the playas of the Black Rock and Smoke Creek Deserts farther south near the present town of Gerlach, also as Mud Lake.[101]

At Lassen's Meadows, Tiffany wrote: "...learned that a Cherokee had come through from California to guide a train of Cherokees & had given the distance on an entirely new route which shortened the road very much avoided the desert at the sink of Mary's River & went through a pass in the mountains without any steep hills to go over, with fine grass & water all the way."[102]

Also at the meadows, Kimbal Webster wrote,

> The other, or right hand road, is called the Cherokee Cutoff, and the distance is said to be but 180 miles to the Feather River gold mines....
>
> The question arose, which of the two roads shall we pursue—follow the old road—the advantages and disadvantages of which we are pretty well informed; or shall we risk the new one...
>
> The question was submitted to a

---

101 In a personal conversation in January 2009 with Jack and Pat Fletcher, authors of *The Cherokee Trail*, they speculated that Dick Owens may have led his Cherokee pack train over this route.

102 Tiffany, Pardon Dexter Diary. Sept. 14, 1849.

> vote of the company, and it was in favor of trying the "Cutoff," as it is called, with scarcely a dissenting vote."[103]

Where the name "Cherokee Cutoff" used for the Lassen/Applegate Route came from is subject to speculation, but it was obviously recorded as such in the journals of later emigrants in 1849.

Earlier, in 1843, a company of Cherokee fur traders, under the command of Captain Dan Coody, traveled to California via the Humboldt and Truckee route.[104]

They wintered at the Johnson Rancho, and when they were returning to the Cherokee Nation in 1844 they met the Stephens-Townsend-Murphy party and gave them information about California.[105]

Some of this knowledge or experience may have later come to play in 1849, as it is well documented that a large contingent of Cherokees traveled from Oklahoma to California in 1849. Various factions traveled by wagon trains and one by pack train. They entered California by different routes.

As the Cherokees traveled north across Colorado into southern Wyoming, they followed an old trappers' trail along the Front Range of the Rockies, leaving their name on what is known today as the Cherokee Trail. Later, when some of them turned off on the Lassen/Applegate Route, it too picked up their name as the Cherokee Cutoff.

While in Pueblo, Colorado, part of Evans party of Cherokees hired Dick Owens to guide them to California by

---

103   Kimbal Webster Diary, Sept. 14, 1849.
104   John Henry Brown accompanied the Cherokees to California in 1843, and his records were published in *Early Days Of San Francisco California*, Biobooks, Oakland, Calif. 1949.
105   *Bancroft History Of California*, pp 732-33.

Nobles Emigrant Trail

the Truckee Route.[106] This group then left the Evans wagon train and became an independent pack train. Capt. Evans later took his followers over the Truckee Route. Although Dick Owens was not a Cherokee, he had previously been in California and was returning leading a Cherokee pack train. He may have been the "Cherokee" that Lord was referring to.

On November 20, Jos. A. Sturdivant wrote a letter home saying,

> *I am now in camp with Wm Shores and Capt Evans, who arrived here about three weeks ago with about half the Arkansas teams. The balance of the train took the northern route on Humboldt River, and my team with them. Learn from Lieut. Rucker who has been with supplies to relieve the emigrants that they had been caught in a snow storm, and have lost all the stock that belonged to the train."*[107]

In *Gold Rush,* Read & Gaines wrote: "It is perhaps not idle to speculate on the routes followed by some of the other Cherokee."[108] It is speculated that Dick Owens, who had been on the trail with Frémont and Carson in 1845-46, led his Cherokee and white packers over the northern route, as they were obviously part of "the balance" of Evan's train, as mentioned by Sturdivant.

The Fletchers and Whiteley, in *Cherokee Trail Diaries,* write that Owens met the party of Amos Josselyn on August 8 and 9 on the Humboldt, and may well have convinced them to take the northern route, as they turned on to it on August 13, "...making no mention of letters, notices, or

106 *Cherokee Advocate,* Aug. 6, 1849; & *St. Jo Gazette,* Nov. 30, 1849.
107 *Cherokee Advocate,* March 11, 1850.
108 Read & Gaines, p. 642.

other inducements to take the route, which were noted by later emigrants."[109]

They also wrote, "It is probable that Owens took his Cherokee and white pack company over a route similar to Frémont's that followed the present Applegate Trail—to Rabbit Hole Springs, then to Mud and Pyramid lakes, and west into California's golden valleys—a route mentioned by Israel Lord."[110] Again, which Mud Lake is being referred to (see footnote #99) would be significant, but going then to Pyramid Lake, as Frémont did, would have led them too far south.

Owens was familiar with the Sierras, as he had been over the mountains with Frémont and Kit Carson in 1845 and 1846. Frémont subsequently named a river, a lake, and Owens Valley in California in his honor. In 1846 Owens fought in Frémont's Battalion of Mounted Riflemen and was captain of Company A. Then, in 1847, he accompanied Frémont to Washington D.C., prepared to testify in defense of Frémont at Frémont's court martial.

As guide to the Cherokee pack train in 1849, Owens was probably as knowledgeable of the route to California as many of the guides on the trail that year.

J. Goldsborough Bruff copied some versions of what he called the "Cherokee Guide" into his journal, listing distances to Mud Lake and High Rock Canyon, but these were essentially based on the Applegate waybill. Bruff also noted that he dined with the Cherokees near Frémont's Castle and in his journal notes he talked of seeing the Cherokees on the trail on several occasions.

Train after train in 1849, from Black Rock Desert on, attempted to find the promised "Cut-Off" either to Feather River or to the Sacramento Valley—among them, McGee

109   Fletcher, Fletcher, & Whiteley. p. 173.
110   Ibid. p. 173.

Nobles Emigrant Trail

himself. William H. Nobles' road from Black Rock Boiling Spring, by Granite Creek Desert, Smoke Creek Desert, Honey Lake Valley skirting the northern sources of the Feather over Nobles Pass, and down to Cow Creek on to Sacramento, accomplished one cut-off in 1851.

The Chiles party had already explored the cut-off from Round Valley (now known as Big Valley) on the Pit River to the Sacramento River in 1843. It was followed by Frémont in 1846, and attempted by Lassen in 1848. But Lassen missed his way. The emigration of 1849 followed, with imprecations of the "long, crooked *Lassin's*" road.

There is some contention that "persons unknown" discovered the Nobles route prior to 1849. Bruff seems to have known of the hot spring at the base of the Selenite Range in the Black Rock Desert, although this spring was not officially discovered until 1856.

Tom Hunt notes this in *Ghost Trails to California* where he writes: "The discovery of this important cutoff is credited to two prospectors in the year 1856, but curiously enough, as early as 1849 Bruff records a report to the effect that these hot springs existed and that a trail just might be possible in that direction."[111]

Read & Gaines wrote:
> The Cherokee were renowned as pathfinders, sharing honors with the Delawares as guides...One might not go far wrong in surmising that Cherokee were among the first converts to take the north trail at the bend of the Humboldt...[112]
>
> It is perhaps not idle to speculate on the routes followed by some of the other Cherokee. Editor Vann, we venture to guess,

---
111 Hunt p. 238.
112 Read & Gaines. p.642.

was one of the *"packers from Pueblo,"* for G. E. Grymes, writing from Sacramento City, Sept. 18, says: *"F. Chisholm and J. Vann are here."*

Dr. Jeter Thompson, leader of the company which took the Independence route, writing from *"Feather River Mines,"* Nov. 1, makes this significant comment: *"Many we hear of still on the road all along for two hundred miles from the settlements, in snow three feet deep."* This describes conditions as they existed only on the Lassen Trail. Did Thompson's party, then, precede Bruff's Cherokees along that route? And how did the *"packers from Pueblo"* come?

One might not go far wrong in surmising that Cherokee were among the first converts to take the north trail at the bend of the Humboldt – a surmise which is arresting in view of its bearing there the name of "Cherokee Cut-off"... One dare not assert, however, beyond the fact that some of those Cherokee of Captain Evans' company who did blaze that other Cherokee Cut-off renowned later as the route of the Overland Mail, did come into California by the Lassen Trail." [113]

Apparently Senora Hicks, a Cherokee, came over the trail with an earlier train in 1849 and was employed by Major Rucker as a guide for the government relief party and later as an advance courier for the Major to carry a circular to the

---

113 Ibid. p. 642.

Nobles Emigrant Trail

emigrants advising them the proceed as fast as possible. It stated, "The bearer of this, Mr. Hicks, has passed over the whole of the route to Lassen's in the valley of the Sacramento, and will give any information to the emigrants that is necessary for the preservation of their stock or their speedy progress." Hicks was first cousin to Major Daniel Rucker's first wife, Flora Coody, who died at Fort Gibson in 1845.

The fact that Hicks was a cousin of Flora Coody suggests that he may have also been related to Dan Coody (also spelled Coodey). Dan was half-Cherokee, and was captain of a party of Cherokee fur traders accompanied by John Henry Brown, a non-Cherokee. They had crossed the country by the Humboldt and Truckee route via Fort Bridger and Fort Hall, spending the winter at what was later Johnson's rancho. Some of the Indians also visited Sutter's Fort. They returned to the Cherokee Nation in the spring of 1844, going eastward. As mentioned before, they met the Stephens-Townsend-Murphy party on the way and imparted information about California to them.[114]

John Henry Brown came back to California in 1845 with the Grigsby-Ide party, and he later published *Early Days Of San Francisco California*, which told of his many adventures.[115]

As Read & Gaines said, "It is perhaps not idle to speculate on the routes followed by some of the other Cherokee," and to wonder if Cherokees may have predated Nobles in crossing his route, and if the horse and mule tracks that appeared to be about ten months old that Bruff saw near Smoke Creek in 1850 weren't from Cherokees passing by in 1849 on the "Cherokee Cutoff," as mentioned on earlier.

---

114 Bancroft. *History of California*, Volume II, p. 732 & 733.
115 Brown, pp. 1-9.

KEN JOHNSTON

Nobles Emigrant Trail

Nobles' Return to Minnesota and Road Promotion

After William Nobles returned to Minnesota, he gained some publicity from promoting his new road and stumping for a route from western Minnesota to California over his new pass into the Sacramento Valley.

In February of 1854, having gained the backing of the Minnesota legislature, Nobles presented his ideas to Congress with the following speech.

Author's note: The lengthy speech covered in the following seventeen pages is a verbatim replication of the passage from Nobles' Emigrant Trail, by Robert Amesbury, which he took from History of Oregon and History of California, H. H. Bancroft Library, San Francisco.

KEN JOHNSTON

"Mr. President:

"In conformity to your request, I will endeavor, this evening, to demonstrate to you the many advantages which an emigrant route to California and Oregon, through this, our favored Territory, possesses over any other route yet traveled.

"Hitherto a route through the Territory, to the golden valleys of California or the luxuriant vales of Oregon, has never entered the minds of emigrants. Our Territory has been regarded as located in the frigid north, and covered with eternal snows, and it was deemed ridiculous to think of penetrating the snows of the North with a view to reaching the shores of the Pacific in the Southwest.

"By reference to the *N.Y. Tribune* of January 14, you will find that by recent arrivals, information had reached New York, that the survey had been commenced. Also in the *New York Evening Post*, about the same date, the following item appears:

> Dr. Wozoncraft and his party had arrived at Sacramento, and were cordially received by a committee appointed by a public meeting to raise funds to forward this work. It is his intention to make a through exploration of this pass, and proceed, if practicable, as far east as the Humboldt river. It is the Doctor's opinion, that this pass has an altitude of 2,000 feet less than any other gap running through the Sierra Nevadas, –even than Walker's Pass itself.
>
> This exhibits the interest felt in California in regard to this important

Nobles Emigrant Trail

subject, and is also an indication of their confidence in the feasibility of constructing a railroad through this route; but however important a railroad route direct from this city to San Francisco may be deemed, there is a subject of more immediate importance presents itself.

Years must roll around before a railroad can be constructed on any route between the Atlantic and Pacific coasts; but in the meantime, there is a flood of travel which will continue to roll across the plains to California and Oregon. To indicate a route by which much of the sickness, hardship and privation which has heretofore attended the overland emigrant, may be obviated, and much valuable time and expense to the emigrant may be saved, is more directly the subject upon which I wish to speak this evening.

"Mr. President, suppose a person to be at Chicago, on his way to California if he wishes to go the old route, he must go from

Chicago to St. Louis	500 miles
St. Louis to Council Bluffs	900 miles
Council Bluffs to South Pass	950 miles
	2,350 miles

"Eight hundred miles of that distance is up one of the most difficult and dangerous streams we have in the West, and proportionately expensive.

KEN JOHNSTON

"Now Sir, suppose we examine the distance by the Minnesota route.

Chicago to Galena	164 miles
Galena to St. Paul	320 miles
St. Paul to South Pass, as in table	<u>800 miles</u>
	1,284 miles

"Making a difference in the distance between the route by the Council Bluffs and that through Minnesota, of 1066 miles, more than equal to the whole distance between St. Paul and the South Pass. The actual difference in land travel being about 200 miles, an important item.

"I had difficulties to contend with in my endeavors to induce the people of California to believe that such a pass as I found existed. It will be remembered that I had been but about two years in California, — that the subject of securing a good pass through the Sierra Nevadas, the most difficult to the emigrant of all the mountain ranges, had been agitated in California; that the old mountaineers of the country had made repeated excursions in search of a more favorable route than those generally traveled, and that after the failure of those men of experience, the announcement that I, a new comer, had discovered a practicable pass, was received with ridicule by the mountaineers, and with deep distrust by the people.

"I will first read from the *Courier* of April 17, 1852, my proposition to a large meeting of the people of Shasta City, in relation to the route:

> *Mr. Nobles said: With the assistance of the citizens of Shasta, I propose to open a good wagon road from this place to the Humboldt river. For the sum of $2,000 I will indicate a route across the Sierra Nevada to the Humboldt*

Nobles Emigrant Trail

river, which will be shorter and in every respect more practicable than any other known overland immigrant route into California. I would charge nothing for making the proposed route were it not for the fact that I have spent some money and much time in making its discovery. If, however, a company is sent with me, and should be dissatisfied with the road when they reach the eastern slope of the Sierra Nevada Mountains, I shall not consider myself entitled to any remuneration whatever.

I propose to take a party that may be selected to accompany me to the Truckee river, by a route which shall not vary ten miles from a direct course. The mountains are easy of ascent, and in no case will double teams be required to accomplish their passage. The snow upon the mountains is not of sufficient depth to prevent the travel of the road during the last portion of the month of April. In no instance are watering places on the route at a greater distance apart than eleven miles, and the grass abundant. The travel saved to the wearied immigrant will be at least two hundred and fifty miles over any other known route.

The point where the line of this route will intersect the Humboldt river is about sixty miles above the sinks of *that river, and very nearly on the same parallel of latitude with this place. From this place to Humboldt river by the proposed road, the distance is not more than two hundred and fifty miles. I have traveled the distance in eleven days, and believe it can be easily accomplished in eight.*

On the route there are many desirable points for ranches, toll-bridges and ferries. If a company is formed for the purpose of opening the road, I shall ask an interest in one point of the road which I shall indicate. If, however, the public should take the matter in hand, they are welcome to all the advantages that may accrue from opening the road.

I now leave the subject in your hands. I do not ask the payment of a cent for making public my route across the mountains, until those whom you may select to accompany me shall say that it is short and practicable for wagons.

"After the meeting had been addressed by several of the most prominent persons in Shasta, it was moved and carried, that:

"A committee of three should be appointed to collect $2000 in subscriptions to forward the objects of the meeting; and that said committee should make it their duty to request persons to accompany Mr. Nobles in opening the road; the committee to report on Monday evening next.

"I will now read from the *Courier* of April 24th, 1852, an

Nobles Emigrant Trail

extract from the proceedings of a subsequent meeting of the citizens of Shasta, on the same subject:

This evening the citizens of Shasta assembled at the St. Charles Hotel, pursuant to previous adjournment. Messrs, Roop and Bonnafield, from the committee on subscriptions, reported that $1600 had been subscribed. During the meeting $75 in addition to the above was subscribed.

The following persons were reported to be in readiness to accompany Mr. Nobles on his expedition: D. D. Harrill, W. Bonnafield, Samuel Francis, Dr. Thomas T. Cabaniss, John Follansbee, Charles Smith, S. B. Knox, John Stratton, and Thomas Sheridan.

"The same paper contains the following editorial on this important subject. It exhibits the deep interest felt by the people of Northern California, on this important subject:

NEW IMMIGRANT ROUTE

In another column will be found the proceedings of two meetings of the citizens of Shasta, held during the present week, for the purpose of considering and acting upon the proposition of Wm. H. Nobles, Esq., to open a new more direct route from Humboldt river into the settled portions of California. Mr. Nobles has offered to indicate a direct route for a good wagon road across the mountains *for the sum of $2,000. It will be seen by the proceedings of the meetings referred to, that $1,676 had been subscribed on Wednesday last. The balance will be furnished before the expedition starts. The company has already been formed and will take its departure in the first of the coming week.*

Northern California has every reason to feel proud of the conduct of the citizens of Shasta and vicinity in reference to this subject. The hope of finding an easy wagon road across the Nevada Mountains has been reluctantly but long since abandoned. Great minds in the east have paused at the foot of these mountains in the advocacy of that opus magnum in National Improvements — the Atlantic and Pacific Railroad — and have finally laid aside their favorite scheme as impracticable.

Those, therefore, who have taken a part in this matter may rest assured that the accomplishment of the present undertaking, as is confidently promised by its projector, is fraught with consequences of incalculable importance, not only to California, but to the whole Union. If, however, the movement should prove to be a failure, the money will be paid back to the rightful owners, and our citizens will still enjoy the satisfaction of knowing that

Nobles Emigrant Trail

they have manifested a commendable disposition to advance the interests of their State and country.

"I will now, Mr. President, read from the *Courier* of the 19th of June, an extract from the report of the party appointed to accompany me through the new pass to the Humboldt river. The party were absent from Shasta about six weeks:

IMMIGRANT ROAD ACROSS THE SIERRA NEVADA MOUNTAINS – MR. NOBLES' ROUTE – RETURN OF THE PROSPECTING PARTY

On Thursday morning last, after an absence of near six weeks, the party that accompanied Mr. Nobles across the mountains, returned to our town. It will be remembered that Mr. Nobles, in consideration of the sum of $2,000, promised to show a route for a wagon road which would be superior in every respect to the routes previously traveled. The members of the party all concur in stating that Mr. Nobles has fulfilled his promise to the letter, and in some respects, even more than fulfilled them.

We cannot give as full a report of the movements of the prospecting party as we could desire – not having sufficient room.

The distance from this place to the point where the road intersects the Humboldt river, is thought to be not more than three hundred miles. It can be easily accomplished in eight days with a pack train. So far as could be determined in the absence of proper instruments for taking latitude and longitude, the route does not vary ten miles from a direct line.

On no part of the whole road are the hills difficult of ascent, traveling in either direction. The road leading from this place into the Sacramento Valley, over which Concord coaches pass daily, is said to be more rugged than any section of the proposed road.

In traveling east from this place after the Sacramento Valley is left, the ascent is gradual and easy all the way to the summit of the mountains – a distance of about ninety miles. After one day's travel from the summit down the eastern slope, which is said to be a gradual and easy descent, the plain of the Great Salt Lake Basin is reached at a place called Honey Lake Valley. From this place to the Humboldt river, eighty miles above its sink, the distance is about one hundred and sixty miles.

This section of the route is almost a perfect level, and is across that strip of country on the east of the mountains known as the Desert. The passage of this Desert by immigrants, with animals worn down by months of travel, has caused their chief sufferings and loss.

Nobles Emigrant Trail

By the proposed road, it is said that this great obstacle in the path of immigrants, will be almost entirely obviated. The greatest distance anywhere between Humboldt river and Honey Lake Valley, where it would be necessary to travel without water, is not more than twenty-five miles.

At all the watering places on this section of the road grass is found, and some places it is very abundant and of excellent quality. Honey Lake Valley is several miles in extent and is watered by three creeks and innumerable springs. It is now covered with a luxuriant growth of grass. Its lands are all exceedingly rich and are well situated for cultivation. Several members of the company took up claims at this place and intend returning within a few days for the purpose of improving them.

This valley will serve as an excellent place for the wearied immigrant to stop with his stock and recover his strength after his long and tedious travel from Missouri. The grazing is sufficient for many thousands of stock for the whole year.

In the passage over the mountains no place was found destitute, either in water or grass.

No stream was found on the whole road that could not be easily forded.

KEN JOHNSTON

In many places on the route, indications of the existence of gold were observed. On the eastern slope, a vast amount of quartz was observed. The party, however, were not prepared with necessary implements, and had not time, and are consequently unable to make any definite report as to the mineral resources of the country over which they passed. It is confidently anticipated, however, that rich deposits of gold will be discovered on the route.

The party remained on Humboldt river eight days. While resting at that place a party of twenty-two men passed on their way to St. Louis from Yreka. With these men Mr. Nobles left his party, and started for his home in Minnesota.

ROAD FROM SHASTA TO HUMBOLDT RIVER
(from the **Shasta** Courier*)*

In another column will be found a brief report of the action of the company of citizens who volunteered to accompany Mr. Nobles in making a thorough survey of a route for a wagon road across the Sierra Nevada Mountains. The exploring party left this place on the 3rd of May, and their return and report have been anxiously awaited. By reference to their report in another column it will be seem [sic] that the anticipations of the most sanguine have been fully verified.

Nobles Emigrant Trail

This road will unite all the advantages claimed for the various other immigrant routes across the mountains. It is shorter, the route being almost on a direct line from Humboldt river to the Upper Sacramento Valley. The suffering and loss of property, occasioned by the poisonous waters at the Sinks of Humboldt, and in passing over long and barren deserts, will be almost entirely obviated. There is an abundance of grass and water for the whole distance.

In addition to these distinctive characteristics of the proposed road, the conformation of the country is such that the passage over the mountains will be comparatively easy. The ascent is not rugged or difficult, traveling in either direction.

While the opening of this road will materially enhance the value of property in the Upper Sacramento Valley, the comfort and health of immigrants will be greatly promoted. Immigrants reaching the settlements by this road will find a delightful valley to welcome them after their toilsome and fatiguing journey. Here they can rest and afford their stock an opportunity to regain their strength.

In speaking of the many advantages of this new road, its eligibility as a railroad route cannot be passed over *in silence. The gentlemen who have been on this route are men in whose representations unlimited confidence can be placed, and from their report we feel convinced that the country over which they have recently traveled will afford the only practicable railroad route across the Sierra Mountains within the limits of California. Should a careful survey and a scientific report confirm the representation which have been made to us, we feel satisfied that the investment of such an amount of capital will be induced as will insure the connection of our State with the Mississippi Valley, by railroad within a few years.*

NOBLES ROUTE TO SHASTA FROM THE PLAINS FIRST ARRIVAL OF IMMIGRANTS
  In another column will be found the names of twenty-six immigrants from Illinois, Wisconsin and Indiana, who arrived in this place on Wednesday evening last, having crossed the Desert and Sierra Nevada Mountains, by Nobles' new Shasta Route. The party came in under the pilotage of A. P. Shull, one of the first surveyors of the route.
  The entire party has expressed satisfaction with this new route across the mountains. Water and grass are abundant. The hills are all stated to be easy of ascent

Nobles Emigrant Trail

and descent, being no where more difficult in their passage than are the Black Hills about Fort Laramie. Those, therefore, who have crossed the Plains, will readily perceive the unrivaled advantages of the Shasta Route.

On other routes, the passage of the Desert between the Humboldt river and the Nevada mountains, is a task of extreme difficulty, involving not only a great loss of stock, but frequently a sacrifice of human life. On the route under consideration, the Desert is hard and smooth, and the distance between watering places is no where greater than twenty-five miles. Grass also abounds in sufficient quantities to sustain stock.

This route also possesses the advantages of being more direct than any heretofore traveled by California immigrants. In pursuing the roads through Carson Valley the immigrant is compelled to travel over a hundred miles almost directly south, over sandy roads, with insufficient grass and brackish and poisonous waters. By Lassen's trail, the sacrifice of time, distance and strength, is even greater than by the southern route. The Shasta route leaves the Humboldt river about 80 miles above its Sinks, and until the head of the Sacramento Valley is reached, it does not vary ten miles from a due west course.

KEN JOHNSTON

"I have endeavored, Mr. President, to lay before this meeting the advantages of an emigrant road through this Territory to Oregon and California, and now hope that the meeting will take such steps as will be most likely to obtain that assistance from Congress, which will secure to the emigrants over the land route a safe and convenient means of transit."

Author's note: This ends Nobles' speech. The following is a continuation of Robert Amesbury's narrative.

Congress eventually passed a bill to grant 300,000 dollars for the improvement of this route which was to be divided into 3 sections, Nobles in charge of the eastern third with 50,000 dollars to work with. Unfortunately, he was severely hampered by Indians demanding payment through their lands and Minnesota land speculators, these last being the very ones who had been so anxious to send him to Congress.

Most Minnesotans were staunchly behind their hero, for on the 23rd of May, 1857, the legislative bill was passed creating the county of Nobles and eight others in the southwestern corner of the territory. It was named in honor of Col. W. H. Nobles of St. Paul.[116]

During 1857 and 1858, the Fraser River gold excitement electrified the nation and in 1858, a meeting was held in St. Paul to promote a northern route to these gold fields in Canada via St. Paul and the Red River. One of the very active participants in this meeting was Wm. H. Nobles.

---

116 Robert Amesbury gives Nobles the title of colonel. It is somewhat confusing that Nobles County was named in honor of Col. William Nobles in 1857, when Nobles hadn't, as yet, served in the Civil War and been commissioned as a colonel. See next chapter for more discussion.

Nobles Emigrant Trail

When they came to select a leader to blaze this new road whom did they select? William H. Nobles, who had in addition to his other pursuits been elected to the fifth Minnesota territorial legislature in 1856 from Ramsey County.

In 1859 an expedition prepared and set out to blaze this new route. That it ended in failure cannot entirely be placed on this man's shoulders for many reasons. First, he was already too busy to have been snared into this hardship. He was only 43, but it was a costly time to be taken from his first love, the Minnesota Honey Lake wagon road.

Also, they started in mid June of 1859, too late in the year to reach the mighty Fraser in Canada and return before the bitter winter that this country offers caught them. It was also said of Nobles that he was unable to hold his party together in the face of developing friction and personal differences. This must be accepted with personal prejudice because had he not possessed to some extent these very qualities and many others of leadership he could never have made his mark on history that he did.

On February 9, 1859 Nobles expressed a desire to close the records of the Ft. Ridgely road but his affairs were turned over to the Attorney General's office, and in June 1860 the United States District Court of Minnesota handed down a decision in the case of United States vs. Wm. H. Nobles awarding the government a judgement [sic] of $3,446 and court costs. The Interior Department charged the road builder with $21,000 of missing property. In the tense weeks before the Civil War, Nobles claimed the department cut off $20,000 in funds and his workers took that amount of supplies in lieu of salaries.

Testimony following this event flew thick and fast and partisan politics were deeply involved. William Nobles

KEN JOHNSTON

was finally exonerated but his management of the whole affair could have been more successful had he not been diverted to the Fraser river during the crucial year of 1859.[117]

In 1862 he entered the Army and was appointed Lieutenant Colonel of the 79th New York Volunteers, better known as the "Highlanders." While on duty in South Carolina a personal collision with another officer led to his resignation. He still served the government, however, first as a cotton collector, U. S. Revenue officer, and master of transportation of troops. At the conclusion of the war, broken in health, he repaired to various mineral springs, finally returning to St. Paul to die December 28, 1876, at the age of 60.

Author's note: This ends Amesbury's quoted portion.

---

117 Amesbury pp. 6-14.

Nobles Emigrant Trail

A Confusion of Names:
Col. William H. *Noble* and
Col. William H. *Nobles*

Since there has been so much confusion among historians and authors about Col. William H. **Noble** (sometimes spelled Nobles), it seems prudent to give some clarification by presenting his biography.

William Henry **Noble** was born in Connecticut in 1813, three years earlier than William H. Nobles, who was born in 1816 in New York state. Mr. Noble graduated from Yale University with a law degree and was admitted to the bar when he returned to his home in Bridgeport. He became the Connecticut State Attorney General in 1846. He was commissioned colonel of the Seventeenth Regiment of Connecticut Volunteers, known as the Fairfield County Regiment.

KEN JOHNSTON

Colonel William Henry Noble
Photo courtesy Roger D. Hunt Collection/USAMHI

Above photo is of William Henry **Noble**, Colonel of the 17th Regiment of Connecticut Volunteers[118]

---

118   Lehman, Eric D. http://bportlibrary.org/hc/barnum-and-related-items/general-william-henry-noble/

NOBLES EMIGRANT TRAIL

The drawing above is the home of General Noble in Bridgeport, Connecticut[119] *Courtesy Roger D. Hunt Collection/USAMHI*

With a thousand men under his command, the regiment fought with heavy losses in the Civil War. Fighting against Stonewall Jackson's forces in Chancellorsville Noble's horse was killed beneath him, and he was shot in the arm severing an artery. He was also wounded in the knee by a shell fragment.

Luckily, his artery clogged, and he was sent home to Bridgeport to recuperate, but he returned to his regiment and to battle before healing completely. He was captured on Christmas Eve of 1864 and was imprisoned as the highest-ranking officer in the notorious Andersonville Prison Camp.

119   Ibid.

After the war ended, he was breveted a brigadier general in the Union Army. He did not serve after the war and returned to Bridgeport to resume his civilian life.[120] After the war he and his daughter made a very comfortable living handling pension claims for Union veterans.

In addition to the confusion between William H. **Nobles**, for whom the Nobles Trail is named, and Col. William **Noble** from Connecticut, other historians have clouded the issue.

William H. **Nobles**
Courtesy Robert Amesbury

---

120 Ibid

Nobles Emigrant Trail

While doing research on William *Nobles* at the Nobles County Library in Worthington, Minnesota, this author found two books published by the Nobles County Historical Society, which gave background on the county's namesake. Both refer to Col. William Nobles and claim the county was named in honor of him.

These two books appear to be so full of errors as to lose credibility, which the author will try to point out.

Raymond Crippen, a local historian wrote:[121]

> Bill Nobles was a wanderer. Born in New York in 1816, he learned the machinist trade and moved west to Wisconsin in 1841 when he was twenty-five, stopping at St. Croix Falls. He helped to build the first mill at that place. He then moved to Willow River (Hudson), Wisconsin. In 1848, when he was twenty-seven, he came to St. Paul.
>
> "Nobles departed for California:1849, gold! Nobles lived in Shasta County and in his travels he hit upon a pass through the Sierra Nevada mountains which came to be called Nobles Pass. Nobles Pass still can be found on California maps; there are people who guess it should be Noble Pass. The Union Pacific railroad laid its track through Nobles Pass. This shortened one emigrant route to California by five hundred miles. Some grateful Californians raised a purse and gave Bill Nobles $10,000 for his discovery.

Note: There are a number of discrepancies in this quote. 1) Nobles didn't go to California until 1850. 2) His pass is in the Cascade Mountains—not in the "Sierra

---

121 Crippen, Raymond. *The Names of Nobles County.*

KEN JOHNSTON

Nevada mountains" as claimed. 3) Nobles never lived in Shasta County; he only approached the people of Shasta City about his new route. 4) There is no railroad through Nobles Pass. 5) It didn't shorten the distance to California by 500 miles, and 6) Nobles only received $2,000 from the people of Shasta city.

Crippen's book continues:

Bill Nobles was forty-five when the Civil War began. He remained in Minnesota for at least the first months of the war; during 1861 he was president of the Minnesota Old Settlers Association. Sometime after this he returned to New York and became a lieutenant colonel in the 49th New York Infantry Regiment for a part of the war—long enough to preface his name with 'Col.' for the rest of his days. After this he held a succession of minor government positions. Col. Nobles suffered several years of ill health and he died at St. Paul on December 28, 1876, at age sixty.

Note: The author has been unable to find any record of William Nobles in the registry of the 49th New York Infantry Regiment.

The second book, *Nobles County History*, edited by Al Goff, likewise states:

Nobles County was established May 23, 1857...It was named in honor of Col. W. H. Nobles of St. Paul, who discovered a pass through the Rockies which shortened the route of the immigrants to the west coast some 500 miles.

There are discrepancies in this short paragraph, also. 1) Nobles Pass was not in the "Rockies"; 2) it wasn't 500

Nobles Emigrant Trail

miles shorter; and 3) if Nobles County was named in honor of Col. W. H. Nobles, when it was established in May of 1857, the Civil War hadn't even started yet, and he wouldn't have been a colonel at the time.

Another intriguing reference as to how William Nobles became a "colonel" appears in Richard Thomas Wright's *Overlanders*. He claims Nobles was a native of New York who became a skilled machinist "who after serving as an officer with General Sam Houston in the Mexican-American War came to the small village of St. Paul in 1848."[122]

Wright gave no reference for where he acquired this information, and the author has been unable to find any evidence supporting this.

Robert Amesbury's claim that Nobles was appointed Lieutenant Colonel of the 79th New York Volunteers in 1862 seems the most credible information. Under the heading "79th New York Volunteer Infantry" in Wikipedia,[123] a list of notable commanders is listed. William Nobles is one of the names on that list.

Additional research found more detailed information. The Unit History Project of the New York State Military Museum and Veterans Research Center, NYS Division of Military and Naval Affairs shows this information on page 989 of the unit roster in the Report of the Adjutant-General of the 79th infantry:

> "Nobles, William H.—Enrolled, to serve three years, and appointed lieutenant-colonel, no date; discharged, December 3, 1861. Not commissioned lieutenant colonel." [124]

---

122 Wright, Richard, *Overlanders*. p. 9&10.
123 Wikipedia, https://en.wikipedia.org/wiki/79th_New_York_Volunteer_Infantry
124 (http//dmna.ny.gov/historic/reghist/civil/infantry/79thinf/79thinfMain.htm)

KEN JOHNSTON

Nobles Emigrant Trail

Epilogue

Although Peter Lassen was perhaps the pioneer of Northern California who explored much of the area and provided information and guidance to many gold seekers and William H. Nobles in1851, it was Nobles who promoted the information and profited from providing a superior route into Northern California and the Sacramento Valley to the merchants of Shasta City.

The route, known as the Nobles Trail, is still the "superior route" into the northern part of the state, but due to the political pull of the more populous areas, it was not chosen as a railroad line or interstate route. The trail remains intact for most of its distance from the Black Rock to Shasta City and can generally be followed by two-wheel-drive vehicles. (Be sure to check road conditions.)

Anyone interested in Western History and the emigrant trails is encouraged to check out Oregon California Trails Association (OCTA) and Trails West, Inc., as they are organizations that promote interest, protection, maintenance, and information about the trails.

Anyone interested in the outdoors and adventure should drive the Nobles Trail and discover the history, mystery, and experiences portrayed in this edition of *Nobles Emigrant Trail*.

KEN JOHNSTON

Nobles Emigrant Trail

About the Author

Kenneth Johnston grew up in Colorado, where he had access to the Rocky Mountains for hiking, hunting, fishing, camping, horseback riding, and enjoying the out-of-doors. He attended the University of Colorado on a wrestling scholarship--winning a National AAU wrestling championship while there. He graduated with a degree in biology and worked as a biologist in the Pribilof Islands in Alaska and as a field assistant in Wyoming doing ethological studies of elk and moose, before serving as an officer in the U.S. Navy during the Viet Nam conflict.

After his discharge, he attended California State University at Chico, where he earned a Masters Degree in Zoology. He has worked as a freelance naturalist and Interpreter for several National Parks and the Museum of Science and Industry in Portland, OR. He served as president of the Klamath Basin Audubon Society for several years and edited their newsletter The Grebe. He served two terms as Captain of the Klamath County Sheriff's Posse.

He is now a retired educator and author. In 2012,

KEN JOHNSTON

he published Legendary Truths: Peter Lassen and His Gold Rush Trail in Fact and Fable, and is currently working on two more books: *Two Boomers on a Beemer*, about his adventures and conjectures of riding his BMW motorcycle with his wife Jo, and *Winnemucca to the Sea, Birding and Biking the Mythological Road*.

Ken has been actively involved with Oregon and California Historic Trails since 1974, when he was hired by Lassen Volcanic National Park to develop a living history program to interpret the development of the Lassen and Nobles Trails, which are closely associated with the Park.

He is presently serving on the board of directors for the California-Nevada Chapter of the Oregon California Trails Association and is president of Trails West, Inc. He continues to enjoy exploring emigrant trails, and traveling the world. He and his wife, Jo live in Klamath Falls, Oregon.

Nobles Emigrant Trail

KEN JOHNSTON

NOBLES EMIGRANT TRAIL

BIBLIOGRAPHY

17thcvi.org: An Online History of the 17th Connecticut Volunteer Infantry During the U.S. Civil War

Amesbury, Robert. *Nobles' Emigrant Trail*. Susanville, CA: Lassen Litho, 1967.

Babcock, Willoughby M. "Gateway to the Northwest: St. Paul and the Nobles Expedition of 1859." *Minnesota History*. Vol. 35, No. 6. (June 1957) 249-262. Saint Paul: Minnesota Historical Society Press Paul: Minnesota Historical Society Press.

Bagley, Will. *With Golden Visions Bright Before Them: Trails to the Mining West, 1849-1852*. Norman, OK: University of Oklahoma Press, 2012.

Bancroft, Hubert Howe. *The Works of Hubert Howe Bancroft*, Volume XIX, History of California, Vol. II. 1801-1824. San Francisco: A. L. Bancroft & Company, 1885.
——*Bancroft History Of California, Pioneer Register and Index*. vol.19.

Barrett, J. William II, ed. *The Overland Journal of Amos Piatt Josselyn: Zanesville, Ohio, to the Sacramento Valley, April 2, 1849 to September 11, 1849*: together with letters,...during, and after the California gold rush. Baltimore: Gateway Press, Inc. 1978.

Beeman, Tam. "Glimpses into Shasta County's Past" a section of "The Bull, The Bear, and Bill Asbury." *Covered Wagon, The*. Redding, CA: Shasta Historical Society. 1973. 72.

Bridgeport Library, Bridgeport History Center. General William Henry Noble. http://bportlibrary.org/hc/ barnum-and-related-items/general-william-henry-noble/

Brock, Richard K. and Robert S. Black. *A Guide To The Nobles Trail: An Emigrant Trails West Guidebook*. Reno, NV: Trails West, Inc. 2008.

KEN JOHNSTON

Brown, John Henry. *Early Days Of San Francisco California*. Oakland, CA: Biobooks, 1949.

Bruff, Joseph Goldsborough. (See Read and Gaines for details)

Bulette, Julia C. Chapter 1864 (see E. Clampus Vitus)

Carlson, Helen S. *Nevada Place Names: A Geographical Dictionary*. Reno and Las Vegas: University of Nevada Press. 1974.

Crippen, Raymond. *The Names of Nobles County; How the Names for the Towns and the Townships, the Lakes and the Streams and the Streets Came to Be*. Worthington, MN: Nobles County Library, 1990.

Covered Wagon, The. Shasta Historical Society, Redding, CA. (Numerous articles cited by author's name)

Dreibelbis, John A. "A Jaunt to Honey Lake and Noble's Pass," *Hutchings California Magazine* June, 1857.

Eggenhoffer, Nick. *Wagons, Mules and Men: How the Frontier Moved West*. New York: Hastings House Publishers,1961. University of Nevada at Reno. 1961

Evanoff, John C. "Deep Hole and Sand Pass." *Nevada History*. www.visitreno.com/evanoff/feb-07.php.2007.

Fairfield, Asa Merril. *Fairfield'sPioneer History of Lassen County California*. San Francisco: H. S. Crocker Company. 1916.

Favour, Alpheus H. *Old Bill Williams, Mountain Man (The Civilization of the American Indian Series)* Norman, OK: University of Oklahoma Press. 1936, 1962.

Fletcher, Patricia K.A., Dr. Jack Earl Fletcher & Lee Whiteley. *Cherokee Trail Diaries*. Caldwell, ID, The Caxton Printers, Ltd,

Fremont, John Charles. *Report of the Exploring Expedition to the Rocky Mountains in the Year 1842; and to Oregon and North California in the Years 1843—1844*. Washington: Gales and Seaton, Printers. 1845.

Nobles Emigrant Trail

Hamilton, William Thomas. *My Sixty Years On The Plains: Trapping, Trading, and Indian Fighting.* New York, Forest and Stream Publishing Co. 1905.

History of Fairfield County. "Noble, Colonel William H." Nobles Regimental History. http://seventeenthcvi.org/blog/history-index/william-nobles-regimental-history.

Hollenbeck, Edna R. "Trees and Graves Mark Site of Canon House." *Covered Wagon, The.* Redding, CA: Shasta Historical Society, 1966.

Holly, George and others. "Upper Feather River Watershed (UFRW) Irrigation Discharge Management Program. Final March, 2007.http://ucanr.edu/sites/ucce-plumas-sierra/files/13633.pdf

Hunt, Thomas H. *Ghost Trails to California.* Palo Alto, CA, American West Publishing Co. 1974

Hutchings California Magazine. San Francisco: Hutchings & Rosenfield, Publishers, 1856-1861

Jackson, W. Turrentine, *Wagon Roads West: A Study of Federal Road Surveys and Constructions in the Mississippi West, 1846-1869.* Berkley and Los Angeles, University of California Press, 1952.

Johnston, Kenneth L. *Legendary Truths, Peter Lassen & His Gold Rush Trail in Fact & Fable.* Greybull, WY: Pronghorn Press. 2012.

Jones, Peggy McGuckian, "Emigrant Trails in The Black Rock Desert: A Study of the Fremont, Applegate-Lassen, and Nobles' Routes in The Winnemucca District." 1980. Reno, NV: United States, Dept. of the Interior, Bureau of Land Management. 1980.

Kurtz, Patricia L. "Mountain Maidu and Pioneers: A History of Indian Valley, Plumas County, California, 1850-1920." Master's thesis Chico State College, 1963.

KEN JOHNSTON

Lehman, Eric D. "General William Henry Noble." 17thcvi.org: An Online History of the 17th Connecticut Volunteer Infantry During the U.S. Civil War http://seventeenthcvi.org/blog/images/william-noble/ Colonel William H. Noble

Lizzio, Ken. *Forty Niner: The Extraordinary Gold Rush Odyssey of Joseph Goldsborough Bruff.* New York: The Countryman Press, 2017.

Lowdon, Scamman. "Memories of Old Shasta (From *The Covered Wagon*, 1950, Written in 1934)." *Covered Wagon, The.* Redding, CA: Shasta Historical Society. 1976. 61-64.

Peninou, Ernest P. "A History of the Sacramento Viticultural District Comprising the Counties of Butte, Colusa, Glenn, Sacramento, Shasta, Sutter, Tehama and Yolo, With Grape Acreage Statistics and Directories of Grape Growers," An Unpublished Manuscript 1965, 1995, 2000 pp. 26 & 27.

Purdy, Tim I. *At a Glance A Susanville History.* Susanville, CA, Lahontan Images, 2005.

Read, Georgia Willis, and Ruth Gaines, eds.*Gold Rush: The Journals, Drawings, and Other Papers of J. Goldsborough Bruff Vol I and II.* New York, Columbia University Press, 1944.
——*Gold Rush: The Journals, Drawings, and Other Papers of J. Goldsborough Bruff.* New York, Columbia University Press, 1949.

Schuler, Carmen. "George Fredrick and Elizabeth Schuler: and Early Days in Eastern Shasta County." *Covered Wagon, The.* Redding, CA: Shasta Historical Society, 1962. 23-31.

Shuford, Beth. "Dedication of Marker on Nobles' Emigrant Road." *Covered Wagon, The.* Redding, CA: Shasta Historical Society. 1969. 5-7.
——"The Story of the Langdons and the Ogburns: as told by Harriet Ogburn Groot, daughter of John and Emma Jones Ogburn." *Covered Wagon, The.* Redding, CA: Shasta Historical Society. 1960. Pp 26-28.

Nobles Emigrant Trail

Smith, Dottie. "Charlies Place Bear & Bull Fights," Travelin' in Time, a weekly look at historic places in Shasta County and the north state. Redding, CA, *Redding Record Searchlight*, March 25, 2011.
——*The Dictionary of Early Shasta County History*. Dottie Smith, Second Edition, 1999.

Southern, May H. "George Furman." *Covered Wagon, The*. Redding, CA: Shasta Historical Society. 1970.

Stewart, David R. "The San Joaquin Historian, The Native Peoples of San Joaquin County Indian Pioneers, Immigrants, Innovators, Freedom Fighters, and Survivors." Part Two. Lodi, CA, San Joaquin Historical Society, Inc. Winter 2016.

Stewart, George *The California Trail*. Lincoln, NE, University of Nebraska Press 1983

Swartzlow, Mrs. Carl "The Noble Trail." *Covered Wagon, The*. Redding, CA: Shasta Historical Society. 1957.

Swartzlow, Ruby Johnson. *Lassen: His Life and Legacy*. Mineral, CA, Loomis Museum Association, 1964.

Trails West, Inc. *A Guide to the Nobles Trail*. (See Brock, Richard and Bob Black.)

Wheeler, Sessions B. *The Nevada Desert*. Caldwell, ID, Caxton Press. 1971.
——Unionville's *Humboldt Register*, April 15, 1865.

Wilson, General John, Letter to Peter Lassen dated Jan. 3, 1849 (probably 1850). Submitted as Exhibit G in Court Transcripts of Charles L. Wilson & John Wilson vs. Peter Lassen & Henry Gerke. Sacramento, CA: California State Archives, October 8, 1853.

Wright, Richard Thomas. *Overlanders: The Epic Cross-Canada Treks for Gold, 1858-1862*. William Lake, BC, Canada: Winter Quarters Press, 2000.

KEN JOHNSTON

NOBLES EMIGRANT TRAIL

INDEX

Symbols

79th New York Volunteer Infantry 275

A

Adams, Horace 135
Airport Road Bridge 209
Allen, Catherine B. 206
Allen grave 153
Allen, Nancy Ann 153
Allen, William L. 206
Alturas 30, 53
Amazoo 83
Amesbury 4, 19, 24, 28-29, 42, 45-46, 60, 69, 79, 84, 91, 93- 96, 99, 114, 117, 140, 142, 144, 146, 148, 160, 179-180, 199, 201, 208, 219-220, 226, 251, 266, 268, 272, 275
Amesbury, Robert 4, 19, 28, 45, 79, 94, 140, 142, 144, 146, 199, 219, 251, 266, 272, 275
Andersonville Prison 271
Applegate-Lassen Trails 51
Applegates 50
Applegate Trail 22, 38, 65, 231, 239-240, 246
Arcularius, Lucius 56, 91
Atlas Obscura 190

B

Badger Flat 161, 235
Bagley, Will 38
Baker, "Doc" 199
Ball Ferry 183
Ball, Harriet 182-183, 194
Ball Mill 9, 183
Ball, W.W. 183
Bancroft, Hubert Howe 190
Bannocks 58
Barnhart, Charles 59
Basin Hollow 206

KEN JOHNSTON

Bath Tub Lake 160-161
Battle Creek 9, 175, 179-180
Bear & bull fights 194
Bear Creek 9, 199, 201
Bear Flag Revolt 35
Beckwith, Lt. E. G. 101
Benton City 32, 217
Bidwell 23, 81, 83, 144-145
Bidwell, John 23
Bidwell, John C. 144
Big Meadows 30, 33, 36, 221, 223, 228, 230-231
Big Spring 9, 149-151
Big Valley 247
Big Wheels 9, 181, 183
Black Butte (Cinder Cone) 9, 160-161, 169
Black Butte Creek 160
Black, Robert S. 26, 223
Black Rock 7, 19, 26, 29, 33, 38, 46, 48-51, 53-54, 56, 63-65, 74, 76, 88, 101, 143-145, 147, 220, 223, 228, 231, 233, 237-238, 240, 243, 246-247, 277
Black Rock Desert 29, 53, 63-64, 76, 220, 233, 237, 240, 243, 246-247
Black Rock mines 144-145
Block 127-128 (See Mud Springs Massacre)
Bloody Point 79, 84
Bogard, John and Rachel 76
Bonnafield, W. 40, 257
Bosquejo (See Lassen's Rancho Bosquejo)
Bradway, Joseph R. 199
Bradway, J. R. 121
Bridge Creek 151, 153
Bridge Creek Spring Road 151
Bridgeport 269
Bridgeport, Connecticut 271
Briggsville 211
Brock and Black 93, 177, 179
Brock, Richard K. 26, 223
Brown, John Henry 244, 249
Bruff, Joseph Goldsborough, J. Goldsborough 4, 23, 28-32, 105, 107-110, 112, 115, 131, 133, 219-220, 222, 234, 246-249
Buck, Don 35, 65, 226
Buena Ventura land grant 213
Buffalo Canyon 97
Buffalo Springs 8, 91, 93, 96-97

Nobles Emigrant Trail

Buljin Gulch 211
bull and bear fights 190
Bull Creek Ranch 121
Bull Springs 121
Bureau of Land Management (BLM) 73
Burning Man 49
Burning of Mud Flat Station 123
Butchery at Granite Creek Station. 54
Butte Creek 9, 159-160, 167, 169, 177, 233, 235
Butte Creek Meadows 159, 167, 169, 177, 235
Butte Lake 160-161
Byers, James D. 147

C

Cabaniss, Thomas T., Dr. 40, 257
calcium carbonate rosettes 62
calcium carbonate tufa 100
Caleb Greenwood 59
California National Historic Trail 38, 232
California Pastoral 190, 193
California Trail 16, 19, 23
California Volunteers 113
Camp Bidwell 81, 83
Camp McKee 53, 59
Camp Pollock 101, 113
Canon house 214
Canon House 10, 211, 213, 214
Carlson, Helen S. 67
Carson, Kit 23, 50, 67, 75-76, 87-88, 238-240, 245-246, 265
Cascade Mountains 273
Castle Creek 145
Catey, Elizabeth Ann 214
Catey, Mr. 213
Catlett, C.C. 33, 228
Cedarville 97
Centerville 211
Central Pacific 148
Chaos Crags 161, 234-235
Chaos Jumbles 14, 163, 234-235
Charley's Ranch 9, 188-189
Charlie's Place 189, 191, 193-194
Charlie's Ranch 9, 189, 194, 197
Cherokee 10, 109-110, 240-249

Cherokee Cutoff (Cherokee Cut-off)10, 109, 240-244, 248-249
Cherokee Nation 244, 249
Cherokee pack train 110, 243, 245-246
Cherokee Party 240
Cherokees 243-244, 246, 248-249
Cherokee Trail 243-245
Chico 92, 143-145, 147, 203
Chiles party 247
Chinatowns 217
Chinese 217-218
Chinese cemetery 217
Cinder Cone (Black Butte) 161-162, 169, 234-235
Civil War 266-267, 271, 274-275
Clear Creek 10, 210-211, 215
Clover Creek 206
Coburn, Vesper 80-84
Cochran, R.M. 144
Colburn, Phoebe 197
Columbia River 32, 225
Comanche 36, 95, 230
Comstock Lode 143
Congress 4, 22, 38, 232, 251, 266
Connecticut Volunteers 269-270
Coody, Dan, Captain 244, 249
Coody, Flora 249
Council Bluffs 253-254
Court Transcripts 33, 36, 222, 229-230
Covel, A.L. 193
Cow (Canoe) Creek 234
Cow Creek 10, 30, 206-207, 209, 222, 234, 247
Coyote Spring 8, 69-71, 233
Creele, C. 56
Crippen, Raymond 273-274
Crooked River 145
Curry, A. 56

D

Davis, Nelson H., Lieutenant 207
Death Trail 22
Deep Hole 8, 58, 78- 84, 91, 113, 145
Deep Hole Springs. 8, 79
Deep Hole Station 58, 78-79
Deer Creek 223

Nobles Emigrant Trail

Deer Flat 9, 166, 177-180, 234-235
DeHaven, W. N. 145
Delano, Alanzo 23
Delawares 247
Derby Lake 131
Dersch, Anna Marie 199, 201-203, 206
Dersch, Fred Sr. 201
Dersch, George 201
Dersch, George and Anna Marie 199, 202
Dersch Homestead 202
Dersch massacre 203
Dersch Ranch 9, 197, 199-200
Dersch Road 194, 197, 205, 207
Devastated Area 161, 234
Devil's Half Acre 169
Dictionary of Early Shasta County History 179
Digger Indians 58-59
Dinosaur 120
Dobyns, Doby 125 (See Mud Springs Massacre)
Donner 21, 239-240
Donner Party 239
Doobie Road 61
Dreibelbis, John 40, 45, 129, 133, 151, 179
Drury Harrill and Co 209
Dry Creek 205
Dry Valley 157
Dye Creek camp 202

E

Early Days Of San Francisco California 244, 249
E Clampus Vitus 133, 193
Edwards, Deputy Sheriff 83
Egan, Ferol 76
Emerson Pass 76, 88, 238
Emigrant Ferry 209-210
Emigrant Ford 161
Emigrant Lake 161
Emigrant Pass 234
Eskimo Hill 166, 171, 235
Evanoff, John 87
Evans, Capt. 244-245, 248
Evans party 244

F

Fairfield, Asa 33, 36, 45, 64-65, 80, 123, 128, 141, 144, 180, 221, 223, 230, 269
Fall River Mills 208
Fariss & Smith 59
Feather Lake 38, 153-155, 233
Feather River 31, 222, 241-243, 246, 248, 281
Fish, Mary 100, 137
Fish, Mary C. 149, 155
Fitzpatrick 67
Fletcher, Jack and Pat 243
Follansbee, John 40, 257
Foot of the Mountain Station 9, 173, 196-198
Fort Bridger 249
Fort Churchill 113
Fort Crook 113, 208
Fort Gibson 249
Fort Granite 59
Fort Hall 242, 249
Fort Kearney South Pass and Honey Lake Road 22, 65
Fort McGarry 54
Fort Reading 10, 38, 194, 207-208, 231, 234
Fox Range 97
Francis, Samuel 40, 257
Fraser river 268
Freeland, John 186
Frémont, John C. 23, 35, 50, 58, 67, 73, 75-76, 87-88, 222, 234, 237-240, 243, 245-247
Frémont, Explorer For A Restless Nation 76
Friends of the Black Rock 74
Frog Springs 69
Ft. Reading 208
Fundenberger, Marvin 14

G

Gaddy, Collins 82
gallows 60
Garrett Ranch 69
Gerke, Henry 33, 35-36, 154, 221-222, 224-226, 228-230, 232
Gerke's home 33, 35-36, 154, 221, 226, 228-229, 232
Gerlach, Nevada 53, 61-62, 73-76, 80, 84, 94, 233, 237, 243
Gerlach Hot Springs 75

Nobles Emigrant Trail

Gerlach, Louis 80, 84
Ghost Trails to California 247
Gillespie, Lieutenant 35, 234
Godey, Alexander (Alexis) 50, 75, 238-239
Godey's Gap 75-76, 238
Godey's Rock 76-77, 238
Godfrey, Grove K. 222
Goff, Al 274
Gold Lake 28-29, 32, 35, 105, 227, 234
Gold Rush 15, 17, 19, 25, 28, 109, 211, 217, 240, 245
Government Road 241-242
Granite Creek 7, 46, 52-56, 59, 63-65, 69, 71, 113, 144-145, 247
Granite Creek Station 54-56, 59, 71, 113
Granite Creek Station Massacre 56
Granite Mountains 73, 84, 95
Granite Point 75
Granite Ranch 64
Granite Range 70, 75
Granite Station 233
Great Basin 93
Great Boiling Springs 8, 68, 73, 75, 237-238
Great Salt Lake 101, 260
Green 126-127 (See Mud Springs Massacre)
Greenhorn 21
Greenwood, Caleb 59
Gridley Springs 145
Grigsby-Ide party 249
grizzly bears 190
Guide To The Nobles Trail A 26, 28, 226
Guill, John 144
Gunsight Notch 120
Guru of Gerlach 61
Guru Road 7, 61-62, 101

H

Hamilton, Lieutenant 135
Hamilton, William Thomas 239
Hammans, Jack 40
Hanging of Charles Barnhart 59
Hanne, Jake Lee 190
Hardesty, Don 53
Hardin City 52

Harper 123, 127
Harrill, Drury D. 40, 167, 205, 209, 257
Hat Creek 9, 161, 165, 167, 169-171, 173-174, 209, 234-235
Hawkins, Lieutenant 242
Heioglyphic Defile 109
Hicks, Senora 248
High Rock Canyon 237, 243, 246
Highway 44 166, 169, 194
Highway 395 129
Hill, Cap. 82
Hill, John 177, 179-180
Hill's Ranch/Trading Post 179
Hines, Fred 64
Hobbs, March 123 (See Mud Springs Massacre)
Hog Flat Reservoir 151
Honey Lake 22, 28, 30, 32, 38, 65, 80, 83, 96, 101, 109-110, 112, 119, 123, 125, 128-129, 131, 133-135, 137, 139-141, 143-144, 151, 154, 219-221, 226, 231, 239, 247, 260-261, 267
Honey Lakers 81-82, 124
Honey Lake Valley 28, 30, 32, 38, 83, 101, 109, 119, 125, 128-129, 131, 135, 139-140, 143, 154, 219-221, 226, 231, 247, 260-261
Hop-we-puck-ee 83
Horn Route 233
Horsetown 211, 218
Hudson, A., General 33, 228
Hudson Bay Trappers 234
Hudson's Bay Company 207
Humbold Register 54 (See also Unionville's Humboldt Register)
Humboldt 38-41, 46, 50-51, 54, 56, 65, 69, 80-81, 114, 123, 125, 128, 139-140, 144, 146, 148, 219, 221, 240, 244-245, 247-249, 252, 254-257, 259-263, 265
Humboldt County Museum 50
Humboldt River 38, 40-41, 54, 65, 221, 245
Humbug Road 149
Hunt, Tom 28, 34-35, 223-229, 247
Hutching's California Magazine 27, 33-35, 133-134, 220, 221, 222, 223, 225, 227, 230

I

Igo 211
Indian Rock 88-89
Indian Valley 27, 31-34, 220-222, 224, 227

Nobles Emigrant Trail

J

Jackass Flat 211
Johnson, Herbert 'Ringtail' 194
Johnson Rancho 244
Jones and Catey 213
Jones, George 213
Jones, Mrs. John 206
Jones, Sydnia 189, 206, 213-214
Jordan Creek Valley 145
Josselyn, Amos 245
Joss House 217

K

Kearny, Stephen Watts, General 239
Keller, George 51
Kellogg 125, 127-128 (See Mud Springs Massacre)
Kimball, Gorham Gates 153, 169
Kingery, Solomon 92, 159, 175
Kingsbury, T. P. 111, 113-115
Kingsbury, William V. 113-114 (See also Smoke Creek Sam)
Kirk, John 93, 100
Kits Peak 238
Klamath Lake 35, 234, 239
Knox, S. B. 40, 257
Kyle, Charles 40

L

Lack Creek Bridge 197
Lake Lahontan 49, 62, 85, 88, 101
Lander, Frederick W. 22, 68, 96
Lassen 4, 13-19, 21-23, 26-38, 46, 50-52, 59, 69, 105, 109, 112-113, 123, 131, 133, 139, 141, 144, 148, 154-155, 157, 160-163, 164-167, 173, 180, 214, 217, 219-225, 227-235, 240, 242-244, 247-249, 265, 277
Lassen/Applegate Route 244
Lassen County Historical Society 131
Lassen Historical Museum 141
Lassen Peak 148, 161, 165-166, 234-235
Lassen, Peter 17, 19, 23, 27-30, 32-34, 36, 50, 52, 105, 113, 139, 167, 214, 217, 219, 221-225, 227-230, 232, 240, 277
Lassen's Big Meadows 33, 36, 46, 69, 221, 223, 228, 230-231, 243

Lassen's Rancho (Lassen's Rancho Bosquejo)32-33, 35-37, 154-155, 217, 221, 222, 223, 228, 229, 230-232
Lassen Trail (Lassen Route) 13, 16, 21-22, 32, 38, 52, 133, 154-155, 157, 221, 223, 229, 232-233, 240, 242-243, 248
Lassen Volcanic National Park 13, 15, 18, 26, 30, 161-162, 164-165, 233, 235
LaTour's Ranch/Trading Post 179
Lawrence, "Comanche George" 95
Lee, J.M. 82, 84
Legendary Truths 23, 27, 222, 225
Liberty Valance 25-26
Litchfield, California 135
Lockhart, Edith 69
Lockhart Ferry 235
Lockhart Road 167, 169, 235
Lockhart, Sam and Harry 167
Lomas 128
Loomis 4, 163, 165-166, 176, 283
Loomis, Benjamin Franklin (Frank) 165, 176
Loomis, Estella 165
Loomis Museum 4, 163, 165
Lord, Israel 23, 241-242, 246
Lost Creek 161, 165

M

malaria 207, 208
Mandeville, J.C. 144
Manzanita Chute 9, 166, 175
Manzanita Creek 175
Manzanita Lake 9, 15, 159, 163, 165-166, 171, 175-176, 234-235
Mapes Ranch 136
Marks, Lafayette 80, 82
Marriott, Samuel 123 (See Mud Springs Massacre)
Mary's River 243
Marysville 95, 143, 149
Masons 32, 214
Masonic signs 127
McCarley and Smith General Merchandise, 186
McCarley, John 186
McCoy, Wm., Sgt. 113, 126-128
McCumber, George 180
McCumber Reservoir 9, 180
McCumbers mill 179, 234

Nobles Emigrant Trail

McGee 240, 246
McIntosh, Elizabeth Ann 214
McIntosh, Frederick 214
McIntosh, Frederick and Rebecca 213
McIntosh, Sydnia Ann 214
McLear, Mrs. M.J. 128
McNamar, Mrs. 201
Messersmith 33, 228
Mexican Land Grant 207
Meyerowitz, Isadore 30
Micheltorena, Governor 213
Middletown 211
Mill Creek 179, 183
Miller and Lux 84
Miller, Joaquin 217
Millseat Creek 180
Millville 9, 203, 205, 206
Millville Plains Road 9, 205
Millville Volunteers 203
Minnesota Honey Lake wagon road 267
Mint Springs 145
Miwok 208
Modoc Indians 239
Mountain Home 179
mountain men 239
Mount Lassen 30, 33, 35-36, 38, 133, 155, 161, 173, 221-223, 229-231, 233-234
Mount Trego 67
Mr. Noble 34, 154, 224, 269
Mr. Pomeroy 35, 230
Mt. Meadows 223
Mud Springs Massacre, 125-128
Mud Flat 121, 123, 126, 128
Mud Flat Station 121, 123
Mud Lake 233, 237, 241-243, 246
Mud Lakes 29, 32, 220, 228
Mud Lakes [Black Rock] 228
Mud Springs 8, 119-123, 129, 145
Mud Springs Massacre 125
Muletown 211, 218
Mullen, John, Major 145, 147
Murder of Partridge and Coburn 80
Murphy and Lawrence 96

Murphy, Frank 95, 96
Murphy's Salt Works 95
Myers, John J. 240

N

Nataqua Territory 113
National Conservation Area (NCA) 50
National Military Road 23
Native Americans 58, 82, 105, 123, 125, 237
Nevada City 143
Nevada Place Names 67
Nevada State Museum 50
Nevada volunteers 113
Neversweats 133
New York Evening Post 252
Noble, William H. (William Henry) Col 269-270
Nobles, William H. 2-4, 7-10, 13-16, 18-19, 21-30, 32-41, 45-46, 49-53, 58, 61, 63-65, 67, 71, 73, 75-76, 79, 84, 87, 91, 93, 97, 99, 101, 105, 109, 111-112, 115, 117-121, 129, 131-133, 135, 138-139, 141-142, 144, 149, 151-152, 154-155, 157, 161-167, 169, 175, 177, 179-180, 189, 194, 197, 202, 205, 209-210, 213, 219-234, 238, 243, 247, 249, 251, 254, 256-257, 259, 262, 264, 266-269, 272-275, 277
Nobles County 266, 273-275
Nobles Emigrant Monument 129
Nobles Emigrant Trail 3, 10, 65, 132, 141, 163-164, 179, 219, 277
Nobles, Lemiel, Rev. 28
Nobles Pass 7, 9, 27, 33, 36, 38, 133, 151-152, 154, 221, 225, 230-233, 247, 273-274
Nobles Second Pass 234
Nobles Trail (also Nobles Road, Nobles Route) 7-8, 13-14, 16, 18-19, 21-23, 25-26, 28, 30, 34, 38, 45, 49-51, 53, 58, 61, 63-65, 67, 71, 73, 75-76, 79, 84, 87, 91, 93, 97, 99, 101, 105, 109, 111-112, 115, 117-121, 129, 131, 133, 135, 139, 142, 144, 149, 155, 157, 161-162, 165-167, 169, 177, 179, 189, 194, 197, 202, 205, 209-210, 213, 219, 223-224, 226, 228, 231-234, 238, 243, 259, 272, 277
Northern Power Company 180
N.Y. Tribune 252

O

Observation Peak 99
O'Connell, David, Pvt. 113
Oddfellow 214
Ogburn Cemetery 182-183, 194-195

NOBLES EMIGRANT TRAIL

Ogburn, Charles (Charley or Charlie) 189
Ogburn, Emma Jones 189
Ogburn family 194
Ogburn, John 189
Old Hill Station, 179
Old Razorback Mountain 67
Old Shasta 10, 215, 282
Old Station 171
Old Summertown 14, 163, 166, 235
Oracle of Gerlach 61
Oregon California Trails Association (OCTA) 19, 277
Oregon pack trail 215
Oregon Trail 16
Oroville 147
Osceola 28
Overland Trail 27
Owens, Richard (Dick) 110, 239-240, 243-244, 246
Owyhee 145, 147
Owyhee River 145

P

Paiutes 51, 56, 58, 109, 203
Paleoindian 49
Parker, Susan 28
Partridge, Hiram L. 80
petroglyph 109, 206
Pierce, Captain 59, 145
Pierce & Francis 59, 145
Piety Hill 211
Pine Creek 155-157
Pine Creek Valley 155-157
Pioneer Program 15, 17
Pit River 235, 247
Planet X 76-77
Platt, Gustav, Pvt. 113
Pleistocene 49-50, 85, 101
Poinsett Creek 167
Poison Lake 156-157, 159
Pollock, James, Pennsylvania Governor 113
Pomeroy, Mr. 35, 222, 230
Pony Express 38, 232
Pool, Bill 201
Poverty Flat 218

Prospect Peak 161, 235
Pruess, Mr. 67
Pueblo 145, 244, 248
Purdom 125-128 (See Mud Springs Massacre)
Purdy, Tim 32, 220
Pyramid 106-107,
Pyramid Lake 73, 76, 87-88, 97, 238-243, 246

Q

Quincy Union 125

R

Rabbit Hole Springs 46, 51, 63-65, 69, 233, 246
Rachford, Christopher C. 80-81
Rancho Bosquejo (See Lassen's Rancho Bosquejo)
Rancho Del Encino 194
Randal, J. D. 52, 175
Razorback 67, 299
Read & Gaines 222, 245, 247, 249
Reading, Pierson B. 183, 207, 211, 213, 215, 218
Reading's Bar 211
Reading's Ranch 218
Red Bluff 147, 149, 167, 210-211, 227, 235
Red Bluff Beacon 227
Red Bluff Road 149
Redding, California 23, 215, 218, 231, 234
Red River 266
Reflection Lake 163
Reid, Robert L. Jr. 202-203
Reno 50, 76, 83, 92, 95
Reynard Siding 97
Robbers Roost 8, 115, 117-119
Rogan, William 59
Roop County 113
Roop, Isaac (I.N.) 8, 113, 139, 140, 141, 145, 150, 257
Roop Post Office 113
Roop's Fort 139-141
Roop Town (Rooptown) 8, 139
Ross, Robert 123 (See Mud Springs Massacre)
Round Valley 247
Ruby City 143-145, 147
Rucker, Daniel, Major 22, 248-249
Rucker, Lieut. 245
Ruggles, Benjamin 135, 151
Rush Creek 101, 115-119
Rush Creek Bypass 119
Rush Creek Canyon 115, 118

NOBLES EMIGRANT TRAIL

S

Sacramento Ferry 10, 209
Sacramento River 183, 209-210, 247
Sacramento Valley 32-33, 38, 143, 151, 154-155, 177, 207, 221, 231, 246, 251, 260, 263, 265, 277
Sage Brush, The 114
Salt Works 94-95
Sand Pass Road 97, 301
San Emidio Canyon 88, 238
San Emidio Desert 88, 238
San Francisco 32-33, 36, 84, 114, 128, 144, 148, 154, 190, 217, 221, 223, 225-226, 228, 231-232, 244, 249, 251, 253
Schuler, Captain 173
Schuler, George 198
Schuler Ranch 198
Scott, Maxwell 25
Sechrist, Laura 53
Selenite Range 247
Shaffer Mountain 136
Shaffer Station 8, 135-136
Shasta 10, 211, 218
Shasta City 10, 16, 19, 22, 26-27, 33-35, 37-38, 41, 139, 143, 148, 210, 213, 215-219, 221, 226, 229, 231-232, 234, 254, 274, 277
Shasta County 125, 179, 181, 197, 203, 205, 215, 217, 273-274
Shasta Courier 38, 40, 201, 215, 262
Shasta Gold Rush 211
Shasta Gulch 211
Shasta State Historic Park 37, 217
Sheridan, Thomas 40, 257
Shingle Camp 185, 234
Shingle Creek 185
Shingletown 9, 176, 181, 183, 185-187, 234
Shingletown Store 186
Shoshoni 58
Shouse, Isaac 189
Sierra Nevada 39, 131, 151, 225, 254-255, 262, 264, 273
Silver City 92, 143, 146
silver rush 52
Simmons, A. 56
Skedaddle Mountains 119, 122
Skedaddle Ranch 119
Smith (no first name) 36, 230

KEN JOHNSTON

Smith, Charles 40, 257
Smith, Dottie 176, 179, 198, 205-206
Smith, Albert 185-186
Smith, John, Pvt. 113
Smith, Raymond 91-92
Smith, William L. (Billy) 197-198
Smoke Creek 8, 10, 30, 32, 38, 59, 73, 75-76, 79, 84, 87-88, 94-97, 99-101, 103, 105-106, 108, 110-111, 113-117, 126, 128, 131, 220, 231, 237-240, 243, 247, 249
Smoke Creek Desert 8, 73, 75-76, 79, 84, 87, 94-95, 99, 108, 220, 237-238, 247
Smoke Creek Fort 59, 73
Smoke Creek Meadows 8, 105
Smoke Creek Sam (William V. Kingsbury) 113-115, 128
Smoke Creek Station 8, 30, 101, 110-111, 114
Snow Buttes 35, 222 (See also Lassen Peak)
Soap Lake 161
Soldier Meadows 52, 54, 144, 145
Soldier's Bridge 135, 137
Spargur, H. L. 125 (See Mud Springs Massacre)
Spencer, 125 (See Mud Springs Massacre)
Squaw creek 80
Stabaek, Tosten Kittelsen 77, 175
St. Croix Falls 28, 273
Stephens-Townsend-Murphy party 244, 249
Stewart, George 23
Stewart, Lucien E. 217
St. Felix 33, 36, 228, 230
Stillwater, Minnesota 28
St. Louis 41, 253, 262
Stockton, Commodore 240
Stone, Sophia Helen 64
St. Paul 226, 254, 266, 268, 273-275
Stratton, John 40, 257
Sturdivant, Jos. A. 245
Summertown (See Old Summertown)
Summit Juniper 168-169
Summit Lake 144-145, 168-169
Sunflower Flat 9, 14, 159, 161-164, 234
Surprise Valley 81, 95, 97, 112, 114
Susan River 38, 129, 133, 135, 137-138, 151, 229
Susanville 8, 19, 23, 32, 38, 54, 74, 79, 82-83, 95, 112-113, 128, 137-141, 143-145, 147-149, 220, 229, 231
Sutter, John 194

NOBLES EMIGRANT TRAIL

Sutter's Fort 183, 249
Swain, Mr. 40
Swartzlow, Ruby 34, 221-222, 227-228
Sweetwater Canyon 88, 238
Symons, Thomas W. 95

T

Table Mountain 171, 234
Taylor, Jobe 32, 34
Taylor, John S. L. 179
Taylor, Ruth Eliza 121
Taylorsville 31-32
Terraced Hills 87
Terwilliger, Phoebe H. 65
Texas Springs 211
Thompson, Jacob 225
Thompson, Jeter, Dr. 248
Thornton, Jesse Quinn 64
Trails West, Inc. 19, 25-26, 47, 50, 92, 96-97, 99-101, 103, 115, 129-130, 135-136, 149, 151-154, 169, 180, 187-189, 199-200, 209-210, 212-213, 216, 277
Trails West marker 50, 92, 96-97, 99, 101, 103, 115, 129, 136, 151, 153, 169, 180, 187-188, 200, 209-210, 212, 216
Trego Hot Springs 8, 64-65, 67-68, 71, 233
Trinitarianus Chapter No. 62 of E. Clampus Vitus 193
Trout Creek 145
Truckee Pass 23, 239
Truckee Route 239, 244-245, 249
Truckey River 241
Tule Lake 239
Tunison 81
Twin Bridges 9, 204-205
Tyrell, Allen J. 111, 137, 185

U

Union Army 272
Unionville's Humboldt Register 56, 283
Upper Reading Springs 215
U. S. Army 59, 112

V

Van Bokelyn, I. L. 33, 36, 228-230
Vance, Richard (Dick) 14

Vary, Ladue 54, 64, 79
View Land 8, 129-133, 135
Viola Resort 9, 176
Virginia City 147
Von Schmidt's 120th parallel 117

W

Wagontown 145
Waldron 56
Walker, Joe 59
Walkers Pass 32, 225, 252
Wall Springs 8, 91-92, 95
Ward, Olin 81
Washoe County 76, 113, 237
Wave cut terraces 85
Wayside Inn 197
Weaverville 217
Webster, Kimbal 243-244
Wells, Almond B., Captain 113
Wells Fargo gold 173
Western Pacific 97
Western Star Lodge #2 Masonic Lodge 217
Wheeler, Sessions B. 56
Whiskeytown 211
Whiskeytown Reservoir 211
White Horse Creek 145
Whiteley, Lee 245-246
Wild Horse Canyon 96
Williams, Bill 239
Williams, DeWayne "Doobie" 61
Williams, Henry W., Lieutenant 113
Willow Creek 138, 145
Willow River 28, 273
Wilson, Charles 224
Wilson, John 33, 36, 222, 224, 229-230
Wilson/Lassen Court Trial 228, 232
Wonder Road 61
Woods, Saschel 217
Wozoncraft, Dr. 252
Wright, Richard Thomas 275

Y

Yana tribe 199
Yerba Buena 33, 154, 232
Young, Ewing 59
Yreka 41, 65, 167, 235, 262
Yuba 29, 220

www.ingramcontent.com/pod-product-compliance
Lightning Source LLC
Chambersburg PA
CBHW070532160426
43199CB00014B/2245